THE RECIPE FOR ECSTASY:

The Couples' Guide to Intimacy and Pleasure

Myrtle C. Means, Ph.D.

Dedication

This book is written for all the lovers, especially mine. Loving and being loved by my husband, Martin Wesley Muhammad (affectionately called Big Daddy) has taught me many things. Most of all, my relationship with Martin has taught me that love alone is simply not enough. Couples must work to ensure the longevity of their bond. Martin constantly works to love me through the many phases of our life. He understands me, accepts me, tolerates me, and celebrates me. For this, I am humbled and grateful. I only hope that what I give him in return approximates the richness he has bestowed upon me. Love is my legacy, I'm glad I get to share it with you, Big Daddy.

TABLE OF CONTENTS

Part Three: Blending Recipes

Part One: Thoughtful Preparation

Ecstasy is a peak emotional experience accompanied by intense sexual pleasure. It represents a time and space in an adult love relationship, a place that every couple should aspire to reach. We can't live there – the variability of life will not allow it. However, our attempts can forever approximate ecstasy. Intimacy and pleasure are key ingredients to the recipe for ecstasy.

HUNGER

The First Bite: Kindling

My experience with couples (and of course my own marriage) has inspired this cookbook for lovers. It is designed to help those who struggle with very common sexual problems, such as low arousal (sex drive), erectile dysfunction, premature ejaculation, performance anxiety, vaginismus, and difficulty reaching orgasm. It is also for those of you who need to add a new twist to an old favorite. This guide will be packed with the nutrients you need for a healthy sexual diet.

New relationships are exciting and full of promise, but they also carry the burdens of insecurity, lack of familiarity and limited shared experience. They may also be afflicted by the throes of excitement, passion, jealousy, and pain that accompany *limerence* – a form of romantic love that overlooks reality, idealizes the partner, and loses all sense of balance. It is the experience of being "crazy in love." According to Masters, Johnson, & Kolodny, (1986) "It is rare for the passion and excitement of a romantic love relationship to last for more than a few years." In relationships that endure, passion and excitement are often replaced by a more mature and stable love. "This is called *companionate love,* which can be looked at as a steadier love based on sharing, affection, trust, involvement, and togetherness rather than passion" (Masters, Johnson, & Kolodny, 1986, pg. 223).

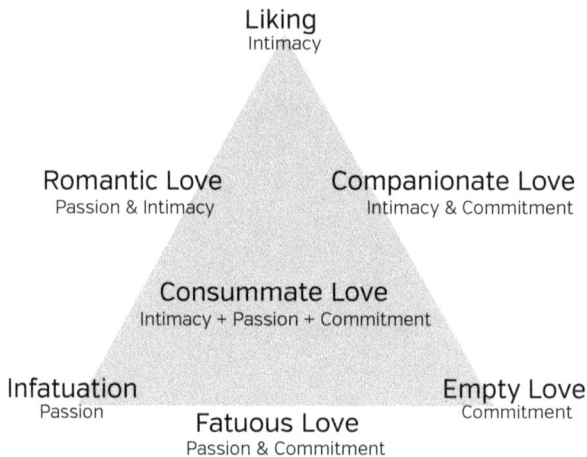

Liking
Intimacy

Romantic Love
Passion & Intimacy

Companionate Love
Intimacy & Commitment

Consummate Love
Intimacy + Passion + Commitment

Infatuation
Passion

Empty Love
Commitment

Fatuous Love
Passion & Commitment

Sternberg's Triangular Theory of Love (1988)

Long-term relationships have the challenge of retaining *intimacy, passion, and commitment.* Sternberg (1988) considers these to be the combined elements of love. Of the three ingredients, passion may be the most difficult to sustain. Some people speak of loving without being in love. Others stay committed for years when intimacy and passion have long since dissolved. These difficulties will inevitably affect the sexual relationship.

In this book, my goal is to infuse stable relationships with the necessary nutrients to ignite passion while staying grounded in intimacy – true love. A love that acknowledges separateness, encourages intimacy, relies on reality, welcomes fantasy (in a creative way that facilitates growth and does not distort reality), and endures the vicissitudes of time.

Sex should be fun. The key qualities of healthy relationships (intimacy, passion and commitment) often bring about fear, frustration, and shame. I want to help couples master the art of lovemaking – in and out of the bedroom. This is not homework. It is the work of life and love. This workbook can be used even during times of conflict in a relationship. For those of you who are living through the common conflicts of marriage (sex, money, and children) this guide will teach how to recover and grow in love. However, it is intended to be a resource throughout the lifespan, during times of conflict and during times of harmony.

While there is a structure throughout this book, it is only a guide. What works for each couple will vary based on unique needs and desires. A virgin couple might have all sorts of questions about the fundamentals of how their bodies function; an aging couple might need to support their ever-changing bodies and interests. Two working parents with children may not have time to devote four days a week to tweaking their *recipe for ecstasy,* while a childless couple may find themselves in the throes of passion several days a week. Keep in mind that this book is intended to accommodate your personal needs and the needs of your respective relationship.

I will walk you through the creation of your very own *recipe for ecstasy.*

This guide can be used in *any* relationship: straight/heterosexual, homosexual/ gay, bisexual, transsexual, or the questioning and curious. The topics and techniques are suitable for any adult romantic relationship. The concepts of intimacy, pleasure, orgasm, fear, rejection, commitment, insecurity, disappointment, forgiveness, inhibition, passion, and variety – these are universal. The partners, preferences and techniques may differ. However, the common objective of adult love relationships binds us. We all want to love and be loved – and to make good love in the process. The only requirement is that you are serious about improving your quality of relatedness. Therefore, some form of commitment or mutual acknowledgment of exclusivity is suggested. True intimacy takes place within a relationship of two individuals who share mutual affections.

While the concepts discussed in this book are universal, narratives have been provided by people in heterosexual relationships. These personal narratives are used to provide examples to the reader of the many concepts being explained. The inclusion or exclusion of certain relationship structures should not diminish the utility of the techniques suggested.

Make this program your own. Use what seems helpful. Substitutions are allowed. It is suggested that you work on your recipe at least twice a week for one or two hours at a time. If you are in for the long haul, what's the hurry? This is not a time-limited experience. Hopefully, you will revisit this book intermittently throughout your time together. It's always fun to play around with new positions, places, and possibilities.

The recipe for ecstasy is not just about addressing problems; it is also about keeping things hot and spicy, creating something new, developing intimacy, and – most importantly – experiencing pleasure. Troubled couples come up with all sorts of reasons to avoid addressing sexual concerns. Anxiety creates a tendency to avert, which, in turn, increases the anxiety. In our sex lives, days turn into weeks and weeks into months of disconnection.

In many ways, sex is like food. Even if you have no appetite, you still should eat. Sex is part of a healthy, loving, adult relationship. Therefore, when feelings of resistance emerge and distract you from cooking up your recipe, I have one word of advice: DON'T! Don't stray from your goal; don't let resistance or distractions get in your way. This is the time to use introspection to understand the urge to avoid. Are you feeling anxious about something? Is there conflict between you and your partner? Don't abandon the work. Use your feelings as a source of information to help you move forward. Find a way to get past the discomfort and resolve conflicts. If needed, get some help from a professional. Tell yourself that you are not allergic to sex, intimacy, or love. It is all natural. You will find a way to enjoy it together, even if you cannot picture it just yet.

The Recipe for Ecstasy will first take you on a personal journey, asking you to consider your history. By exploring your lessons in love, sexuality, and relationships, each partner will also become familiar with their bodies, thoughts, preferences, feelings, fantasies, and fears. The ultimate goal is to discover the ingredients that create *your* personal *recipe for ecstasy,* so that you can share your wish list with your partner. As you learn about yourself, it is important to focus on the process rather than the end goal. Good sex *may* produce orgasms, though that is not the sole objective. If you follow these instructions, orgasms should be, both, powerful and plentiful. I have to tell you though, when two people commit to mutual pleasure and invest in creating intimacy, making love yields far more than an orgasm—it yields ecstasy.

Acquired Tastes

As you move closer to understanding your body and its desires, you will also be charged with learning about your partner. This is an opportunity to ask questions and create a dialogue that you will hopefully maintain throughout the course of your relationship. There may be times during this process when you reach an impasse; conflict may arise.

One common area of conflict results from the different ways males and females approach intimacy and sexuality. Women are complicated. We like to have options. What hits the spot tonight might leave her wanting tomorrow. Women operate from a top-down perspective. She wants her mind and heart stimulated before her body. It is often through an experience of closeness that she feels hot and ready. Men, conversely, are simple. Skip the decadence. Just make sure it is juicy and hot. Men operate from a bottom-up perspective. He, quite literally, would like to see her bottom – up in the air – before he feels close to her. Finding a way for these approaches to compliment each other may be challenging. It may take the form of *her* keeping in mind his desire to get right down to it, while *he* takes the initiative to slow down and cuddle afterward.

Another source of conflict results from the intended purpose of sex. Individuals have unique expectations when they engage in the sexual act. People desire closeness, reduction of sexual tension or other anxieties, the achievement of sexual pleasure (sometimes brought about by the experience of orgasm), comfort, or the validation of self-esteem by feeling desired. Whatever your pleasure, stay mindful of the importance of *mutual* gratification. Know what your partner wants and needs.

Sexuality should be a fluid part of the relationship. People are forever changing while life is constantly evolving. One aspect of this includes sexual preferences and capabilities. Sexual relationship should reflect one's reality and reality should be reflected in the sexual relationship. Intimacy should not be relegated to the bedroom, physically or metaphorically. When two people are lovers, there should be outward signs that are visible to those who view your interactions from a distance. There will be something in the way you smile at him, or the way you admire her, that illuminates the bond between you.

Sexual satisfaction during life's varied circumstances requires situation-appropriate expectations. Think about the different levels of responsibility and flexibility across the life span, such as being a college student, establishing one's career amidst parenting children, adjusting to chronic illness in mid-life, or retirement. The integration of varying life events into love-making recognizes the multiple purposes for sex. This can involve sex one time for anxiety release through orgasm, another time for calm affection amidst fatigue, another time for escape and fun, another for emotional healing, and still another time using sex as a spiritual experience (such as having gentle and tender sex while sharing sadness about the death of a loved one). Satisfying sex is integrated into the couple's daily life and their daily life is integrated into their sex life to create the couple's unique sexual experience (Metz, 2007, 359).

The Temperature is Rising

It is important to understand your bodily response during the sexual response cycle. According to Masters and Johnson (1966), the sexual response cycle has four phases: excitement, plateau, orgasm, and resolution. Take into consideration that Masters and Johnson have focused only on the physiological aspects of sexual stimulation. Sexual expression and responsiveness, however, are likely to reflect the interaction of several things, including health, individual personality, psychological development, and psychosocial context.

The sexual response cycle is as follows:

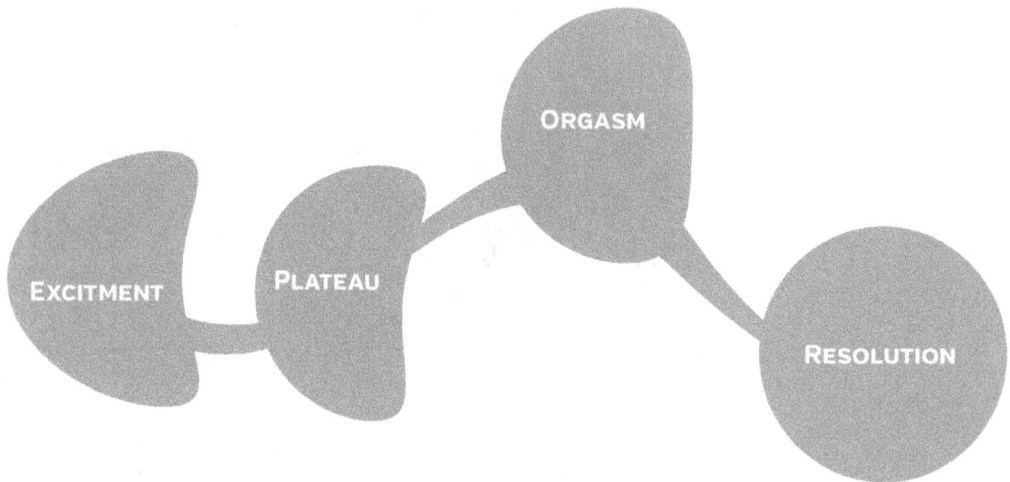

Excitement is the first phase of the sexual response cycle, which is characterized by a number of responses common to both men and women. It may vary from one minute to several hours. Although the stages of the sexual response cycle are the same for men and women, there is a significant difference at the beginning and end of the cycle.

Consider excitement and arousal for men and women as akin to the difference between a microwave and a conventional oven. Arousal in men may only take a few seconds to several minutes, characterized by penile swelling (hardening and expansion of the penis) leading to an erection. The early female physical changes include a slower warm-up and nuanced cooking: vaginal lubrication, vaginal expansion, and swelling of the external genitalia. This phase is also characterized by muscle tension, increased heart rate and blood pressure, engorgement of sexual anatomy, and sex flush—pink or red rash on the skin, usually the chest or breasts. Sexual arousal in men and women is also characterized by a subjective (non-physical) experience of sexual excitement and pleasure.

Plateau is the second phase of the sexual response cycle, in which sexual tension continues to escalate until it reaches the peak (i.e., orgasm). The pot is starting to boil. It is difficult to distinguish this phase from the excitement phase, because there are no clear differentiating signs. This phase lasts a few seconds to several minutes. Prolonged sexual tension during this period may result in greater levels of arousal and more intense orgasms. The heart rate and blood pressure continue to rise; the breathing rate increases; sex flush and coloration of genitals becomes more pronounced; and muscle tension continues to build until orgasm is achieved. In an instant, the pot can go from boiling to boiling over.

Orgasm is the shortest period of the sexual response cycle, usually lasting only a few seconds. But for some of us lucky women it can go on ... and on .... Male and female orgasms tend to differ in a few ways: ejaculation, length, and multiples. Most women do not, but some women are able to ejaculate. They tend to be in the minority, just like men who have the ability to have multiple orgasms. The female body can produce another orgasm immediately following an orgasmic experience.

Female orgasm usually lasts longer than male orgasm. However, the subjective experience of orgasms for men and women are indistinguishable. This phase is characterized by a climax of sexual pleasure variously associated with rhythmic contraction of the perineal and reproductive organ structures, cardiovascular and respiratory changes, and a release of sexual tension. Increased levels of oxytocin (a pituitary hormone) during sex may be implicated in orgasm intensity, as well as subjective experiences of intimacy. Oxytocin is considered the "love hormone." It binds.

Resolution is the final phase of the sexual response cycle, characterized by the return of the sexual systems to a non-excited state. If no additional stimulation occurs, resolution begins after an orgasm. Most men enter a refractory period, a time in which they are unable to achieve an orgasm. The refractory period may range from minutes to days, depending on factors such as age and health. Women, however, are capable of reaching orgasm at any point during the resolution phase.

There are several things that affect the Sexual Response Cycle: age, mental health, fatigue, hormone levels, weight, alcohol/drug use, physical health, medications, and smoking. Therefore, it is important to take stock of the things that could potentially interfere. Adults who experience sexual dysfunction should see a medical professional to rule out or treat underlying health problems. Additionally, a mental health professional may also be necessary to offer education, consultation, and to help resolve sexual conflicts.

What's one to do with this information? Work to understand what makes your body respond. Notice muscle tension, breathing patterns, heart rate, vaginal lubrication, firmness of erection, nipple engorgement, changes in skin tone (sex flush). What genital stimulation arouses you? Explore your erogenous zones. Remember that these are not just your sexual parts. Erogenous zones are all over our bodies and differ from person to person. Explore your elbows, your toes ...who knows?

IN THE PANTRY OF TOP CHEFS

When creating a recipe, you've got to have the right ingredients. People can be particular when it comes to their taste for sexual pleasure. Therefore, individuals must know how to satisfy their personal palates.

Other times, however, seek inspiration and take the advice of those who have perfected the formula. There are personal narratives throughout this workbook to illustrate aspects of sexual and relationship satisfaction. These narratives originated from responses to a survey. I asked 272 women and men to: *"In as much detail as possible, please describe the most sexually satisfying experience of your life."* Respondents also described their sexual partner, including various aspects of the relationship and sexual experiences. [See Appendix A]. Look for **Ingredients**; they were extrapolated from the narratives to identify the key elements that create a unique *Recipe for Ecstasy.*

Pleasure

fantasy

LOVE

devotion

KINK

Ecstasy

Desire

Orgasm

Warmth

Affection

EXCITEMENT!

GROCERY LIST

The Essential Ingredients for Sexual Satisfaction

Mood. . . . . Playful, freaky, relaxed, romantic, anticipatory, satiated

Setting . . . . Awayness, audience potential or presence

Newness . . . . Person, place or thing (sexual act, position, toy)

Variation in the Sex Act . Oral sex, accessories, role-play, sexual positions

Nature of Relationship. . . Committed or casual

Positive Self-Regard. . . . . Good feelings about self or partner

Love . . . . Strong affection (intimacy, passion, and commitment)

Intimacy. . . . . Emotional closeness

Engendered Feelings . . . . Feelings evoked by partner

Passion . . . . Intense physical and emotional response

Arousal. . . . . Physical and subjective excitement

Orgasm Intensity. . . . . Strength of orgasmic response

Multiple Orgasms . . . . Orgasms occurring in quick succession or over time

Communication . . . . Verbal and nonverbal cues

Technique . . . . Sexual skill or ability (The "how" of the sex act)

Timing . . . . The point of occurrence (The "when" of the sex act)

Sexual Abandon . . . . Uninhibited sexual freedom, "kink"

Mutuality. . . . . To give and receive pleasure simultaneously

His focus on her. . . . . Male giver, female receiver

Her focus on him . . . . Female giver, male receiver

HEIRLOOM RECIPES

The Original Chef and Sous Chef

Our preparation for life-long loving takes place from birth. Our love capacity starts with the love that we received from our primary caregivers during infancy and childhood.

> ... something goes on between an ordinary baby and ordinary mothers and fathers that creates and ensures the capacity for love in infancy and in later life. It tells us that love and pleasure in the body begin in infancy and progress through childhood and adolescence to a culminating experience, 'falling in love,' the finding of the pertinent partner, the achievement of sexual fulfillment (Fraiberg, 1971).

For many of us, our first love is the center of the universe, known as "Mother." Although Father is an important piece of this pie, his role is usually secondary to the role of mother.

The Good Enough Mother

A loving mother provides love, warmth, structure, discipline, guidance, comfort, and a sense of value. Passed down to us like grandmother's sacred recipe, "Mother" gives us the sweetest gift – the first ingredients in our *recipe*. Every mother's goal should be to provide the necessary ingredients to produce a person who feels special, valuable, confident and, most of all, loved. When a person knows their value from birth, it is obvious. A foundation in love manifests itself in self-esteem and self-worth, in confidence and hope. It might start with make-believe. For example, young girls and boys may pretend to be princesses and superheroes, respectively. An emotionally healthy girl matures into a woman who demands to be treated like a queen; the boy becomes the hero who wants to honor and protect his most valued treasure.

I have been talking about the "good enough" mother. That is a concept first coined by D.W. Winnicott (1953); he describes her as the mother who *tries her best.* She takes care to make sure that we can care for ourselves. She loves with intention, but has her flaws and, at times, she disappoints. If this vital relationship with mother is befitting, we can be vulnerable, trust and achieve intimacy. Erikson (1963) tells us that a favorable outcome in babyhood yields the inner quality of trust (over mistrust) in the outside world. *Trust* is the foundation for intimacy. Either we achieve it or live in relationships that are characterized by distance.

Unfortunately, there is another kind of mother: the insufficient mother, who neglects, deprives, and abuses. For various reasons, she is harsh, cold, distant, inconsistent, and unavailable. She, too, passes down family recipes. But the outcome is much different. There are no sweet smells to savor. Rather, an offensive odor lingers into adulthood: shame, insecurity, anger, fear, low self-worth, anxiety, avoidance of intimacy, sexual dysfunction.

A mother's impact is indelible. There is no greater influence on our capacity to give and to receive.

Good Enough Parenting

Good enough parenting has nutritive value, providing a person with a paradigm for giving and receiving love. We are nurtured in many ways. Some *direct*, via communication, comfort, guidance, and support. Others are *indirect*, through modeling behaviors. One of the most profound examples of indirect nurturing is the relationship we witness between our parents. This should be one of your first lessons in love. Parents, by way of their interaction, demonstrate how to appropriately express sexual rapport.

Unfortunately, sexuality is often avoided, disregarded, or ignored. Why, when it is as normal as eating and sleeping? Having the opportunity to witness affection, communication, conflict, partnership, intimacy, and commitment is invaluable. The opposite is also true. When there is not a framework in place to teach a child about loving relationships, the child is at a serious disadvantage and will presumably be unprepared for the world that awaits.

If modeling adult love is an *indirect* nutritive provision, then providing loving care to a child is the *direct* nutritive gift that has life-long returns. To "make love" as an adult, you need to be able to create an experience of strong affection, warm attachment, and attraction. Parents provide these key ingredients to babies by way of nurturance. Born helpless and vulnerable, babies need unwavering commitment, the guarantee of intimacy, and to be loved passionately.

If this need is not met, the self is malnourished; it is like being starved to death. Death is the extreme consequence of emotional deprivation, neglect, and abuse. We often think of death as a physical ending of life. However, the death I am referring to is the death of the "self." The more common consequence of neglect – failure to thrive – is a condition that is characterized by delayed physical and emotional development. It has many determinants, is often the result of medical problems, malnutrition, neglect, poverty, or abuse. For our purposes, I will focus on the emotional stunting that occurs and manifests as a result of neglect and abuse (poor nutrition).

Poor Nutrition

Did your parents teach you about sexuality? Did you have a discussion about your body, its development, and its sexual appetite? Did anyone talk to you about intimacy, both physical and emotional? If the answer to any of these questions is "no," you are not alone.

Poor relational nutrition may result in a failure to develop key elements of the personality such as the ability to self-regulate, plan, cope, and develop meaningful relationships. Emotional malnourishment may manifest as poor self-esteem, feelings of inadequacy, poor body image, hopelessness, and sexual dysfunction. The emotionally malnourished individual fails to develop a sense of worthiness, feels unworthy of love. This yields empty relationships.

When a girl is malnourished, she will be insecure, feel inadequate, and have low self-esteem. Thus, she grows into a woman who acts out of desperation. She is unsure of herself and this uncertainty leads to poor mate choices and unstable relationships. When a boy is malnourished, he, too, feels inadequate. As an adult, he will not recognize his strengths and may recoil from the competition of mate selection. Instead, he looks to his sexual conquests for a sense of power and may tend to avoid the vulnerability of intimacy because it provokes feelings of weakness. His penis becomes his sword as he slashes through life, leaving much heartache and pain in his wake.

Why Does a Chef need a Sous Chef?

Intimacy is all about being close. The more you share, the closer you become. "One-der-full" is the experience of oneness and fullness that accompanies true intimacy. Intimacy is grounded in dependency, where one condition or state of being relies on another. Dependency is the true need of a living thing, something that must be present in order for a being to thrive and survive. It is something that a person cannot provide for him or herself. During childhood we experience the greatest level of dependency. In its original form, dependency characterizes the infantile needs for mothering, love, nourishment, warmth, shelter, and safety.

Over time, maturity (which is cultivated by guidance, nurturance and development) creates a change in our needs. We are capable of doing more and, subsequently, need less. However, no matter how much we mature, some needs go unchanged. Thus we are challenged with finding someone who will commit to the gratification of our most enduring need – our need to feel connected.

These narratives provide great examples of **intimacy** and feeling needed or desired.

> *"One of the main things was, he said and did all of the right things. He just knew how to touch and caress me. I didn't have to tell him 'no, not that way,' or 'do it this way....'" I also loved the way he would look into my eyes and tell me how attracted he was to me – overall, how special and needed I was to him."*

> *"... she teased and seduced me. We made love six times during the night. What made this experience so satisfying? I think the fact that this beautiful attractive woman wanted me. Each time we made love it was an intense orgasmic feeling, each time, for both of us."*

The natural state of dependency (the core of intimacy) assumes vulnerability: being without adequate protection, susceptible (open to being affected). A state of being in which a person's guards are down, vulnerability leaves us open to various possibilities – some good possibilities, some not so good. Vulnerability is something that many people avoid because it provokes feelings of weakness and fear. Despite the risks, vulnerability is the only condition that allows for intimacy and growth.

Sexual fulfillment is one way we experience intimacy. Kaplan (1974) contends that emotional closeness facilitates orgasm responsiveness, which, in turn, affects sexual satisfaction. This tells us that the closer two people are, and the more that they share with each other, the greater their chances for sexual satisfaction. Sounds like a *recipe for ecstasy.*

As our abilities grow and our needs change, we should make the transition from total dependence to *mutual interdependence* – a relationship where self-sufficient individuals get their needs met by each other. In adult love relationships, this includes a person's need for tenderness, emotional support, and a sense of attachment. It may also include physical, financial, or spiritual gratification. Mutual exchange strengthens, both, the individual and the union. Here, a man writes about an experience of **mutuality** that creates ecstasy.

"My wife is very beautiful, sensual, and we share a high level of interest in each other which makes our sex life very intense."

Chef or Sous Chef?

In your current love relationship, decide who is the Chef and Sous Chef. The Chef is the one who leads the charge when it comes to the sexual relationship. This person is often the initiator, the person with the higher sex drive, the one who encourages variety and adventure. If there is no clear way to differentiate, then you can choose arbitrarily: flip a coin, arm wrestle, pull straws, play strip poker. This label will be yours throughout our project to distinguish the work being done.

_____ is the Chef.

_____ is the Sous Chef.

STOCKING THE PANTRY

Any great meal begins with thoughtful preparation. You need the key ingredients, the appropriate tools, and an atmosphere conducive for creating your masterpiece. Think about your preparation for loving relationships. What was in your daily diet? Were you properly prepared to give and receive love and pleasure?

Ask yourself these questions:

- Were you nurtured or neglected?
- Were your parents attentive or abusive?
- Did someone talk to you about your body and sexuality?
- Did you have the opportunity to witness loving relationships?

While reading, consider the effects of your personal development in your current relationships, with a focus on sexual satisfaction. Were you deprived, maintained, or nurtured? Keep in mind: deprivation destroys, maintenance maintains, and nurturance nourishes.

Inventory: What's in Your Pantry?

Individuals who enter adult love relationships have plenty of differences between them. These differences emanate from various sources. Our separate backgrounds provide the foundation for these differences. Some people are born into families that provide a strong foundation of intimacy, communication, trust, and sexuality. These individuals make a relatively smooth transition into adulthood. Others are born into circumstances that may be less nurturing – rigid, judgmental, and maybe abusive. Our first relationships leave an indelible imprint on our hearts and minds, and have a considerable impact on future relationships.

Take a moment to identify your personal history and your current role in creating and maintaining closeness in your relationship. Deal with reality. Too often, people concentrate on their anxieties and fantasies. While anxiety and fantasy will not be ignored in our project, they are not the focal point. Now is the time to look at the reality of sexuality and relationships, to find existing and potential pleasures.

On the following pages, I will walk you through an inventory of your sexual history, designed to help you notice what has shaped your current sexual nature, wants, and needs. Reflect on the lessons learned and how they have subsequently impacted you, your sexuality, and your relationships. Your partner will also complete this questionnaire. You will then collaborate on bringing your ingredients together to make a magnificent, *shared*, recipe for ecstasy.

Keep in mind, this is a shared workbook. Each person should consider their level of comfort using the workbook, itself, to document the completed activities. Couples who want their responses to remain private until they feel comfortable with sharing may choose to use separate journals. This may be decided ahead of time or may change throughout the course of the workbook. This is your recipe, give yourself permission to have it your way.

SEXUAL HISTORY: MALE PARTNER

Describe your lessons in love and sexuality. _____
_____
_____
_____
_____

At what age did your puberty begin? _____
• Describe your memory of puberty. _____
_____
_____
_____

Did you masturbate? Yes ____ No____
• If yes, at what age did you masturbate the most? _____
• If no, why not? _____
_____

Who explained puberty/ sexuality to you? _____
• How old were you? _____

What is your religious background? _____
• What implication has it had on your sexuality?_____
_____
_____
_____

Do you recall having significant guilt, conflicts, or mixed feelings related to sexuality? _____
_____
_____

Do you recall any positive experiences that have shaped your sexuality? _____
_____
_____

How old were you when you first started dating? _____
When were you first aware of your own sexual interests? _____
How old were you when you first experimented sexually? _____

Do you have a history of sexual trauma/rape? Yes _____ No_____
• If yes, how has this impacted your sexuality and relationships?

_____
_____
_____
_____

USE THE NEXT SECTION TO DESCRIBE YOUR CURRENT SEXUAL RELATIONSHIP AND SEXUAL PREFERENCES.

Do you currently masturbate? Yes _____ No_____

In your couple which role is yours? Chef _____ Sous Chef _____

How often do you engage in sexual play with your partner? _____
• Are you satisfied with the frequency of sexual interaction? Yes _____ No_____

What is the most gratifying aspect of your sex life? _____
_____
_____
_____
_____

What things would you change about your sex life? _____
_____
_____
_____
_____

Describe any current problems expressing your sexuality or during sexual intercourse. _____
_____
_____
_____
_____

What themes come up when you fantasize about sex?_____
_____
_____
_____
_____

SEXUAL HISTORY: FEMALE PARTNER

Describe your lessons in love and sexuality. _____
_____
_____
_____
_____

At what age did your puberty begin? _____
• Describe your memory of puberty. _____
_____
_____
_____

Did you masturbate? Yes ____ No____
• If yes, at what age did you masturbate the most? _____
• If no, why not? _____
_____

Who explained puberty/ sexuality to you? _____
• How old were you? _____

What is your religious background? _____
• What implication has it had on your sexuality?_____
_____
_____
_____

Do you recall having significant guilt, conflicts, or mixed feelings related to sexuality? _____
_____
_____

Do you recall any positive experiences that have shaped your sexuality? _____
_____
_____

How old were you when you first started dating? _____
When were you first aware of your own sexual interests? _____
How old were you when you first experimented sexually? _____

Do you have a history of sexual trauma/rape? Yes _____ No_____
• If yes, how has this impacted your sexuality and relationships?

_____
_____
_____
_____

USE THE NEXT SECTION TO DESCRIBE YOUR CURRENT SEXUAL RELATIONSHIP AND SEXUAL PREFERENCES.

Do you currently masturbate? Yes _____ No_____

In your couple which role is yours? Chef _____ Sous Chef _____

How often do you engage in sexual play with your partner? _____
• Are you satisfied with the frequency of sexual interaction? Yes _____ No_____

What is the most gratifying aspect of your sex life? _____
_____
_____
_____
_____

What things would you change about your sex life? _____
_____
_____
_____
_____

Describe any current problems expressing your sexuality or during sexual intercourse. _____
_____
_____
_____
_____

What themes come up when you fantasize about sex?_____
_____
_____
_____
_____

SHARING YOUR PANTRY

Effective **communication** is an essential ingredient in your *recipe*.

The sharing of thoughts, feelings, and experiences that accompanies the growth of intimacy in order to learn about each other requires spending time together without the ordinary barriers with which people protect their privacy. Thus, one of the key steps in developing an intimate relationship is self-disclosure, the willingness to tell another person what you're thinking and feeling (Masters, Johnson, Kolodny, 1986).

When you talk to someone directly, you benefit from, both, verbal and non-verbal cues. However, it is not always easy. Choose the path of least resistance. You or your partner may not be ready for this form of intimacy. Check in with each other to gauge if you need to start with baby steps (written communication) or if you are ready to talk openly in person. There will be plenty of time to develop the skill of face-to-face communication. The most important thing is to get started. Therefore, share in a manner that is comfortable for you.

Listen as this woman clearly articulates how the level of **communication** facilitates the process of **arousal** and **intimacy**.

> *"We lay awhile, just stroking and talking. We ended up having a long, intimate conversation about sex. We shared personal histories, laughed, and reassured each other that what we were doing now was fine. We kept stroking and asking each other, 'Do you like this?' 'How does this feel?' Pretty soon I was telling him that it felt really good – we were looking into each other's eyes – 'How's this?' Soon he was exploring my labia, clitoris, and entrance to my vagina – still looking and still asking. Each advance, we went slowly and checked in, always feeling and talking with our eyes and faces. I began to feel incredibly aroused. When his penis came in me, we went slowly, still checking, although part of me wanted to go wild. We ended up making love for a long time, still checking with each other every time we tried something new."*

Here is a woman who knows how to ask for what she wants, and – fortunately – she has a partner who cares enough to give it to her. They were both seeking and giving information. It sounds so basic, yet many people fail to do it. **Communication** is a pathway to **intimacy**. Start by sharing your history.

Sometimes we don't even need words to convey how we feel. This person incorporates **newness**, **intimacy**, **non-verbal communication**, *and* **positive self-regard** in a lovely *recipe for ecstasy*.

> *"It was the first time I'd gazed into my partner's eyes while making love, knowing that he cared how I felt and wouldn't go anywhere unless it felt good to me. That wordless communication marked the rest of our sexual life together. I felt reaffirmed, desirable, and respected and liked just for myself. I loved the communication."*

Remember this is your recipe; choose intentionally. A shared journal, blog, phone conversation or email may assist in relieving anxiety or fears about sharing. You could also leave little notes in special places. This may be a prelude to foreplay or a playful way to initiate sex.

Share Your Secret Ingredients

Independent Study. Use the space provided to decide what to share about your history and how to share it.

Chef's Notes on Sharing Sexual History...

_____
_____
_____
_____
_____
_____
_____
_____
_____

Sous Chef's Notes on Sharing Sexual History...

_____
_____
_____
_____
_____
_____
_____
_____
_____

Sharing Makes it Taste Better

It is important that couples have shared values, dreams, and **meaningful moments** to solidify their bond. *Meaningful moments* include parenting tasks, leisure activities, household responsibilities, and grief. Sex is one of many mechanisms that can also be used for this purpose. If there are problems in the bedroom, people tend to avoid using sex as an ingredient to enrich intimacy. If this is characteristic of your relationship, then it may be necessary to start with some other, less anxiety-provoking, things to share. Take a walk together. Hold hands. Talk to each other. If your sexual relationship has not been spoiled by sexual dysfunction, then the following pages should be considered a way to maintain intimacy over the lifespan.

Every couple should be able to rely upon sharing time together, an inherent part of intimacy. When a person can depend on their partner to create meaningful life experiences, a trust develops. Being dependable with small things solidifies the belief that you will be available to each other for *all* things. Your presence provides a unique experience of closeness, companionship, and partnership.

Often in my work with couples, time and financial limitations are obstacles to spending time together. To get over such hurdles, the menu includes easy-to-implement suggestions, ones that you can create in the comfort of your own home.

Sometimes, though, it is necessary to go outside of your normal routine. For those that don't have limitations of time, money, or children, feel free to indulge. Get creative and splurge. Whatever your pleasure, be sure to share.

Carve Out Time

During a lifetime of sharing, a long-term relationship will experience many phases. There will be periods of great connection and phases when couples feel disconnected from each other. There are several factors that contribute to distance. It may simply be the fact that life gets busy, or it may be something more threatening: conflict, resentment, or betrayal.

A lover's absence creates longing. When this occurs you may find yourself immersed in technology, TV, work, or the distraction of the day – all veiled attempts to fill the void or disguise feelings of emptiness. Turn to each other instead. Whatever the source of distance, be mindful of the need for resolution and reconnection. If you want your relationship to last, put in the time and do the work to remove the space between you.

Intentional time – the time that you designate for **meaningful moments** – is essential to the *recipe for ecstasy*. Our time on this planet is not endless. If this is your one and only life, how will you spend your time? Hopefully, making the love you want.

A solid relationship is not built overnight. Be tolerant, yet persistent. Time is the one thing that you need and will never have enough of. Whatever the method, be sure to carve it out.

In these next two examples, the couple did not *wait* for the right **time**. They made it happen!

> *"After a date night of dancing and just having a good time, we drove to a quiet place and had sex in the car. It was exhilarating and we had so much fun. We had oral sex first and it led to a very satisfying experience."*

> *"In the car after the club in an alley in DC … we didn't give a f!@k and we hounded and pounded 'til we both came. Then took it home for round two. All night … damn! I miss her!"*

Fusion Cuisine

Here are some suggestions for sharing *meaningful moments*. Feel free to add to this list.

- Watch your favorite show. If you don't have a show in common, alternate who chooses the show for the night.
- Take dancing lessons privately or in a group (e.g. waltz, ballroom, hustle, stepping).
- Pick a book of shared interest; take turns reading to each other.
- Play games that you enjoy: Scrabble, Dominoes, Spades, Eucher, Uno, Butt-Naked Twister.
- Pick a sports game, buy the tickets, and experience the crowd.
- Train for a marathon or exercise together.
- Learn a foreign language together.
- Cook together.

COOKING CLASS ASSIGNMENT.

Use the space provided to create a list of *meaningful moments* you would like to share:

Chef's Notes on Creating Meaningful Moments...

_____
_____
_____
_____
_____
_____

Sous Chef's Notes on Creating Meaningful Moments...

_____
_____
_____
_____
_____
_____

KITCHEN CLEANUP

Identify the Expired Ingredients

You have begun to share your history and take inventory of your personal needs. Now, it is time to stock the pantry and make sure that you have an environment that is prepped for menu planning. Before you spend time creating your *recipe for ecstasy*, make sure to tidy up. This can be done alone (introspectively) or jointly (to build connection). Use this time to think about the old wounds and conflicts that need to be cleared out. In the midst of doing this, things may get dirty. Sometimes, through good self care and caring for your relationship, painful or overwhelming thoughts and memories might arise. Trust that, at the end of this work, you will be left with the right conditions to create your ideal feast.

Arguments that *are* productive serve the purpose of bringing individuals closer. Each person gets an opportunity to express their feelings and an opportunity to see things from the other person's perspective. In the end you may find yourself closer to resolution and each other. Couples who never fight are not talking about the things that matter. You can't be close if you are not dealing with your differences. At the same time, couples that are often embattled can't be close either. No one wants to be close to someone with whom they are in constant conflict.

Maybe the expired ingredient is dishonesty which breeds distrust. Yes, we all have things that we will never share with our partners. Everyone is entitled to private thoughts and feelings, but subterfuge and duplicity are a poisonous pair. For example, Masters and Johnson (1974) specifically address the role of deception when it comes to intimacy. "Pretending or faking are euphemisms for lying, and lying divides people. This is especially true in bed." In this instance, a lover is deprived of the information needed to give pleasure. If ecstasy is the goal, then honesty is required. This holds true for sexual problems and preferences, as well as overall relationship satisfaction.

Of course, there are various deceptions that occur in relationships. People hide personal struggles like depression or financial problems. Someone might not disclose their need for more "alone time." Unresolved guilt, shame, and anger can serve as an obstacle to intimacy and trust. Attempts to hide true feelings often manifest as inappropriate action. Unlike feelings, behaviors are public. Take stock of your personal contribution to the problems (harsh words, broken promises, misunderstandings, poor communication patterns, selfishness) and apologize. Do the work to make the necessary changes so that your relationship can flourish. Keep in mind that change will be incremental. It comes in small portions.

Clear Out the Pantry

Every relationship has conflict. However, all conflicts are not created equal. Differentiate between the minor irritants and the allergens that threaten the life of your union. Determine what battles are worth fighting, hash it out, and be done. This section may not have the same relevance for everyone. Take care not to unnecessarily make a mess. Don't dig up conflicts that have already been resolved. Once you have identified expired food, you don't bring it back into your pantry. The same goes for resolved conflicts – once processed, let it go. Harboring resentment about past disappointments may lead to recurring conflict and distance. Forgive. Sometimes people hold on to feelings well past the expiration date. So, your assignment today is to do a thorough inventory and discard what you don't need.

It might be the same fight that crops up over and over and over again. Could it be that this is the one thing about your partner that just won't change? Appreciate the consistency. At least you know with whom you are dealing. Accept the reality and learn to live with it. If you want something different from your partner, ask for it. This doesn't guarantee satisfaction, but it increases the odds. The worst that will happen is disappointment. Lovers will disappoint each other, both in and outside of the bedroom. It is inevitable. There has to be room for recovery.

Because of the difficulty associated with this task, I will leave the medium of communication to your discretion. Just do it – any way you can – by email, mutual journal, letter, whatever works for you. *The only options that are off limits are via text message or social media.* Social media is public and brings the potential for external input and additional problems. I have several couples that use text messaging to fight their battles. It often leads to misinterpretation and exacerbation. Text messaging can be impulsive. Process your feelings and take the time to compose a thoughtful message.

Too Many Cooks in the Kitchen

In my first book, I have a chapter entitled "Don't Shit Where You Eat." That is, don't bring the mess of extra-marital affairs, lying and cheating into your relationship. Couples are supposed to commit to the fulfillment of each other's needs, including the need for sexual satisfaction. Masters and Johnson (1974) assert that sexual satisfaction is related to commitment. They write:

> *If either or both of them must seek sexual satisfaction with other partners, the circle of commitment will have been broken. The more satisfactions they find with other people, the fewer satisfactions do they need from each other; and the less they need from each other, the easier it is for them to go their separate ways. Beyond all rationalization, extra-marital affairs would demonstrate two things: first, that they were incapable of meeting each other's most basic physical and emotional needs, and second, that they did not consider each other unique, and therefore irreplaceable, sources of satisfaction and pleasure (p. 254).*

If betrayal occurs, there is damage to the relationship that needs repair. One way to start the healing process is to have an "open book policy." The person responsible for breaching the trust needs to be transparent. Transparency means full personal disclosure. Where you are, what you are doing, and with whom. Grown ups usually don't like this type of accountability. But it may be necessary to repair the damage. This transparency can't go on forever. The offended person needs to work towards a place where they trust and believe in things unseen. This is easy to do when the offender exhibits genuine remorse, openness, warmth and commitment. The offender has to be honest, humble and tolerant, creating an atmosphere that supports forgiveness. Grief and recovery are a process, a very difficult process that takes time and continuous investment. This process may require the assistance of a professional.

There are other ingredients that should also be left out of your *recipe for ecstasy.* As previously mentioned, everyone has flaws, however, some are more rancid than others and have the potential to do great harm. Sometimes these traits take on a life of their own and you may feel as if you are dealing with a different person. Things such as addiction, violence, intolerance, hypercriticism, and recurring infidelity are all restricted from the list. If these ingredients burden your relationship you likely need assistance that is beyond the scope of this workbook. Seek help!

Take out the Trash

COOKING CLASS ASSIGNMENT.

Use the space below to identify the expired ingredients. Take some time to reflect on how unresolved conflicts have created distance and turmoil between you and your partner. Agree together to remove them from the pantry, now and forever. Big things like affairs and sexual dysfunction should be handled carefully. Some additional assistance may be required for couples that struggle with the tasks of conflict resolution, forgiveness, and moving on (which often requires grieving). You may need to hire a cleaning crew (seek professional help). A couple may enlist the support of a therapist, clergy, or personal advisor. Come clean about these issues and then take out the trash. This type of vulnerability can clear a path for passionate reconnection.

> *"My fiancé and I had broken up and I had not had any other sexual contact since our breakup and when we got back together there were so many emotions going on that it was the best sex ever."*

Chef's Notes on Expired Ingredients...

_____
_____
_____
_____
_____
_____
_____

Sous Chef's Notes on Expired Ingredients...

_____
_____
_____
_____
_____
_____
_____

NATURAL REMEDIES

Anger as an Aphrodisiac

Sometimes, when anger enters the relationship, it is difficult to access feelings of love. Love and anger can and should exist simultaneously. Anger is a source of information like any other emotion. It does not have to manifest in destructive behavior or detachment.

Anger can facilitate intimacy when it is expressed productively. Disclose in a manner that is palatable. Listen with the intent of understanding. Remove judgment and defensiveness. When two people are in conflict, there can be distance. If you communicate in the aforementioned manner, conflict can lead to resolution, and intimacy.

Letter to Your Lover

Too often, couples dwell on the hurts of the past and are remiss when it comes to creating new loving memories. The only way to make room for new memories is to grieve the old. Why are you holding on to a painful past anyway? These memories only serve to create a wedge between you and your partner.

INDEPENDENT STUDY.

Write a letter to your lover. What are the things you should have said long ago? This is your opportunity. You are allowed to be angry, sad, disappointed, and afraid. However, it is the last time you will mention the affair, lie, broken promise, betrayal, or absence (that happened umpteen years ago). Choose your words carefully. Remember that the intention is not to hurt the other person or to dig up old stuff. Instead you are closing a chapter, clearing the stale items from the pantry, and making room for a new harvest.

Chef's Notes — Key Ideas for My Letter to My Lover...

_____

_____

_____

_____

Sous Chef's Notes — Key Ideas for My Letter to My Lover...

_____

_____

_____

_____

Fasting

Abstinence after a fight can aid in the prevention of confusion, allow time for the information to digest, and create time to initiate the process of forgiveness. Not a passive act, forgiveness is an undertaking that requires time and effort. It is intentional and requires work. Take some time to sit with your feelings. During this period, abstain from sexual interactions. This does not mean you should avoid physical contact or expressions of affection. Remember to spend **intentional time** making **meaningful moments** [see p. 29-31] and using **ingredients for pleasure** [see p. 58]. During this time, expressions of affection are especially important. Focus on reconnecting, kindness, and comfort. This may take the form of cuddling, hand-holding, foot massage, gentle caressing, and intimate kissing.

How long do you wait? You decide together. In the meantime, proceed with Menu Planning and Dinner for One. These exercises will offer an opportunity for self-reflection that may assist in your recovery process. If you are struggling, you may also use Dinner for Two as a means of reconnecting.

Hunger Pangs

INDEPENDENT STUDY.

Use this time of abstinence for self-reflection. There may be some difficult moments. If you are not ready to share them with your partner, use a private journal for your personal thoughts and feelings, or use the space provided. You may feel lonely, insecure, or even afraid. Keep in mind that feelings are an important source of information. Stay attuned to how you feel and make a note of it. For example, "I feel lonely when...," or "I am afraid you won't forgive me."

Chef's Notes on Self Reflection...

Sous Chef's Notes on Self Reflection...

Always Compliment the Cook

Complaints can add fuel to a fire that is already raging; during difficult times, be mindful of what you say and how the messages are delivered. One of the positive things about being in a mature adult love relationship is that we do not have to say everything that comes to mind, especially if the timing is bad. Hold on to some of those conversations until the relationship is in a better place, when emotions aren't so high. Or just keep it to yourself. Remember you do have the right to private thoughts and feelings. Tolerate the frustration of having to eat your words. The feeling might just pass. If it is something of significance, it will not disappear and you can discuss it at a more opportune time.

During this period of abstinence, focus on the good things in your relationship and each other. Try to find the time and space to reconnect. Compliments are one thing that people can't get enough of. Like condiments, they could add a little flavor to your recipe. Feed each other positive thoughts and feelings. Be kind and loving. Even if you are biting your tongue to keep from cycling in an unhelpful conflict, you can always find kind and loving things to say to your partner.

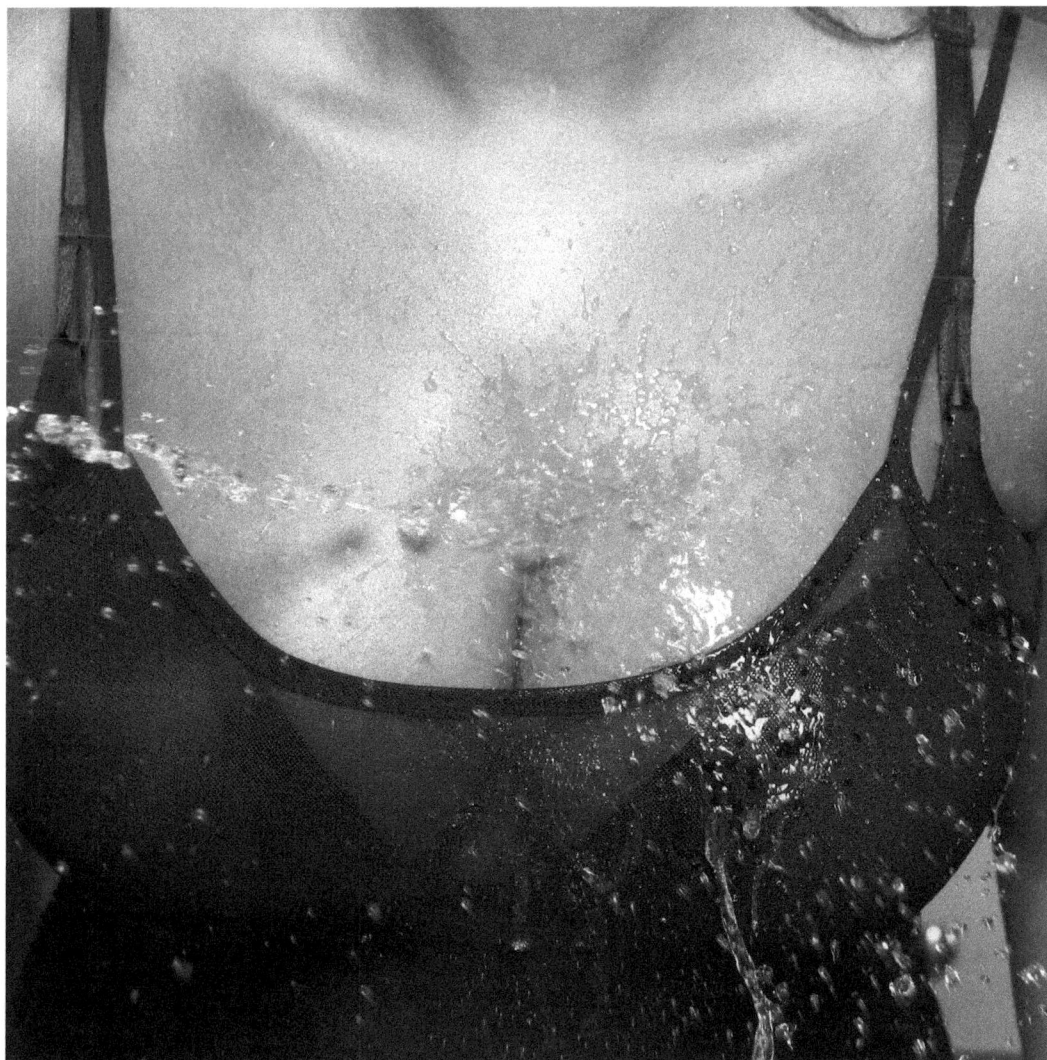

Show a Little Tenderness

INDEPENDENT STUDY.

Think back to the time and space when your relationship was in a better place. List the good things in the relationship and about your partner. Use this to create a list of nice things to say and do during a bad patch. Then show a little tenderness. This can be done by spoken message and/or direct physical contact.

Chef's Notes on Things I Love About You...

_____
_____
_____
_____
_____
_____
_____
_____
_____

Sous Chef's Notes on Things I Love About You...

_____
_____
_____
_____
_____
_____
_____
_____
_____

Chef's Notes on Things I Love About Us...

_____
_____
_____
_____
_____
_____
_____
_____
_____

Sous Chef's Notes on Things I Love About Us...

_____
_____
_____
_____
_____
_____
_____
_____
_____

CHEF'S GROCERY LIST

Kind Things I Can Say or Do,
Even if I'm Angry

SOUS CHEF'S GROCERY LIST

Kind Things I Can Say or Do,
Even if I'm Angry

Comfort Food

Find healthy ways to recover from disagreements, disappointments and disasters. These conflicts (that all couples will experience) come with varying degrees of turmoil. All fights are not created equal. Everything is not a big deal and some things are monumental. We should respond accordingly. Keep yourself in check. Is your reaction proportional to the offense? Allow room for things to improve.

Once it is all said and done, take some time to recover. Each individual may need to do this separately before they can reconnect. Here is another opportunity to be selfish. There may be times when lovers are not able to comfort each other. Sometimes you need your own sweet treat (literally). Pick something that does not have negative consequences that may lead to further distance (such as drugs, alcohol, shopping, overeating). Talk to a friend, get some couch time (see a therapist), take up a hobby, pray, meditate, journal, or exercise.

Share your Comfort Food

INDEPENDENT STUDY.

List the things that help you make it through difficult times. Find ways to share what comforts you. Look for common comforts. Identify what comforts your partner; consider how you can support each other in finding individual time for comforting activities and how you can possibly share a comforting activity. When you implement these strategies, you are beginning the process of individualizing your *recipe for ecstasy*.

**CHEF'S
GROCERY LIST**

Things That Comfort Me

**SOUS CHEF'S
GROCERY LIST**

Things That Comfort Me

Part Two: Knowing Your Appetite

PROBLEMS IN THE KITCHEN

One respondent wrote about his peak sexual experience:

"Probably masturbation, I've never really enjoyed sex with a partner,"

If you can relate to this experience of sexual satisfaction, then you are most likely living with a sexual dysfunction or disorder. The next several pages will provide useful tools to help you understand and work through this challenge.

Sexual Disorders and Dysfunction

Sometimes we encounter difficulties with sexual performance.Through my clinical practice, I am aware that individuals want to resolve this as quickly as possible. Unfortunately, sexual problems must be dealt with in bits and pieces. Sexual exploration (Sexploration) is the first step to gaining awareness about the types of touches that bring you pleasure (see p. 51-58). This same knowledge allows you to effectively educate your partner. The information gathered will be useful in treating women who struggle with *low sexual arousal, anorgasmia* (lack of orgasm), *Dyspareunia* (painful sex) and *Vaginismus* (a condition that makes sexual intercourse impossible or painful due to involuntary contractions of the outer one-third of the vagina). Personal pleasure work can also be useful in treating sexual problems such as *erectile dysfunction* (inability to maintain erection), *pre-mature ejaculation* (not having voluntary control over ejaculation), and *retarded ejaculation* (difficulty producing ejaculatory response).

When dealing with a sexual dysfunction, it is okay to be self-centered Stay focused on your specific sexual and emotional needs. This is one of the rare times in adulthood where being selfish is not only permitted, but also encouraged. There will come a time when your partner should be educated and included in this process, but not yet. Take your time and learn about your body and mind. Take note of any negative thoughts that may be intruding upon your sexual experience. The mind-body connection is undeniable and can have a strong influence on sexual responsiveness.

Women especially need to let go of the culturally supported idea that sex is for men. Reject the idea that to be a lustful woman who wants more than intimacy or reproduction makes you a whore or perverse in some way. Men should set aside the idea that sexual prowess is connected to your manhood. It will only serve to perpetuate the experience of performance/spectator anxiety. Sex is a natural bodily function, like eating and sleeping. Enlist all of your senses to gather information about how your body responds to various types of stimulation. Use the personal pleasure massage (Sexploration) as a foundation for understanding the obstacles to sexual gratification.

Once you have successfully completed the here-and-now experience (see p. **56**) that allows you to gather information without distraction, feel free to use sex toys and other accessories, such as video or auditory stimulation, to facilitate arousal. Fantasy is another tool that may support sexual responsiveness. Let your mind go and be free of worry about performance, fears of rejection, desires to please others and feelings of inadequacy. Top yourself off with the sights, sounds, smells, touching and tastes of personal pleasure. Ultimately this work will lead to climax.

Sexploration work is a means to improvement of overall sexual health. If you experience the aforementioned problems, take this opportunity to work on strengthening your sexual awareness and responsiveness. Note that sexual problems often requires the assistance of a multi-disciplinary team of professionals such as urologists, endocrinologists, psychotherapists, and sex therapists. It is important to rule out any medical causes of sexual dysfunction. Therefore, a medical professional should be consulted. Don't be afraid to ask for help.

Techniques to Address Male Sexual Problems

Erectile Dysfunction. Erectile dysfunction (ED) is one of the more common sexual problems that men face. ED is defined as a persist inability to attain and maintain an erection sufficient for sexual activity. Causes can be psychological (anxiety, depression, trauma), behavioral (drug use, smoking, obesity), and physiological (medication, prostate surgery, injury, aging). There are also several different treatments for this sexual dysfunction. If the cause is medicinal or behavioral, the corrective measure is simple. Consider other medications or change the maladaptive behavior. Sometimes, however, ED requires a more involved treatment approach.

For men who can achieve an erection, but have difficulty maintaining it, the use of a penis ring (also referred to as cock ring) may alleviate the problem. This mechanism is placed at the base of a flaccid penis. After arousal, it slows the flow of blood out of an erect penis, resulting in a longer duration of erection and heightened pleasure. There are several pharmaceutical treatments, including the use of testosterone gel (i.e Androgel), penile injections, and/or erectile dysfunction medications such as Cialis or Viagra. Other treatments options for ED include the penis pump and penile prosthetics. The type of treatment may be connected to the source of the dysfunction. For a more complete review on treatment options for ED see *Appendix E: Erectile Dysfunction is Not a Death Sentence.*

Premature Ejaculation. Treatment of premature ejaculation often relies on training oneself to identify and control levels of sexual responsiveness. *Squeeze technique, stop/start technique, edging, and repeated peak training* are different terms to describe a process where a man self-pleasures to the point right before orgasm (plateau phase). Once plateau is reached the level of arousal is allowed to decrease by stopping the stimulation being provided. Squeezing just beneath the head of the penis or squeezing near the base of the penis can disrupt the sensations of pleasure. You may also simply remove the source of stimulation. When the urge to climax has subsided, self-pleasuring is resumed. A male should repeat this process 3 to 5 times per session before allowing himself to reach the next stage: orgasm.

Men experiencing premature ejaculation may need several attempts before they identify the point where stimulation should be removed. Don't get discouraged if you erupt before the desired time. Continued practice will help a man improve his understanding of how his body works and, thus, gain better control. Remember there is no mastery without error or practice. Be patient with yourself and practice, practice, practice. Exercises help improve sexual functioning in several ways: building stamina, improving hardness, increasing bodily awareness, and strengthening orgasmic response. With enough practice, this process trains the body and brain to gain control. Don't forget the secret ingredient – Kegels (see p. 60).

Desensitization and distraction are two other methods that will help delay ejaculation. Desensitization may be achieved by wearing a condom or by slapping the penis against your thigh or the favorite body part of your partner (buttocks, thigh, face and mouth). Be mindful that the purpose is to reduce sensation. Some men find this slapping sensation very exciting. Therefore, if you are getting more aroused than you should be, stop. Distracting yourself from the sexual experience may further assist in reducing the level of sensation. Feed your mind with images and ideas that are not arousing (count backwards from 100, lyrics to a favorite song, or the grocery list). Be careful not to think of things that will create anxiety, such as the bills. You want to decrease the level of arousal momentarily, without creating problems regaining an erection.

There are also pharmacological treatments available to delay ejaculation. SSRI class antidepressants have been prescribed for premature ejaculation. Their usefulness may be two-fold. SSRIs address the anxiety that often affects this response and a side effect of this medication is delay of the ejaculatory response. Dapoxetine, (Priligy) is a short-acting SSRI medication that has been developed strictly for the treatment of premature ejaculation. At the time of this publication, it has not yet been approved by the FDA.

Techniques to Address Female Sexual Problems

Low sexual desire. Limited interest is one of the most persistent sexual problems faced by women. A person's sexual response builds on the previous stage. Arousal is the first stage of the sexual response cycle, is affected by desire. Lack of interest often results in problems with arousal, and this subsequently leads to problems with reaching orgasm. Therefore, it is essential that a woman takes time to understand her physiological and emotional response to various methods of stimulation. Problems with desire, arousal, and difficulty achieving orgasm can be related to many factors, including age, hormonal shifts, medications, overall health, relationship problems, *mood*, fatigue, or alcohol and drug use. It is important for a woman to rule out any medical causes of low sexual desire. Therefore, early consultation with medical professional is recommended.

Vaginismus. If you are dealing with *vaginismus*, personal pleasure work during *Sexploration* (see p. 51) should be done before the use of dilators or digits (fingers) into the vagina. Here, the objective is to remain relaxed as you and, subsequently, your partner progressively dilate the vagina. It is also important to emphasize the need for humble expectations. Working through vaginismus requires patience and understanding. In this instance, sexual intercourse is prohibited until you successfully progress through the stages of dilation without pain or emotional distress. There may, however, be some discomfort. This specific condition requires the support of a multidisciplinary team of professionals. Physical therapy for pelvic muscle work and/or medication to reduce pain may also be warranted.

Dyspareunia. Painful intercourse can have many causes, both psychological and physiological. Pain during sex is often secondary to other conditions including vaginismus, menopause, endometriosis, allergic reactions, inflammation, and vaginal infections. Dyspareunia may also result from psychological distress associated with sexual abuse or trauma. There may be some simple solutions such as: ensuring proper arousal with more foreplay or the use of a personal lubricant (Replens or Astroglide); identification and removal of allergens; or relaxation techniques. Medicinal treatments may consist of addressing the underlying condition with physical therapy, medication, and/or surgery. Non-medical treatments would focus on resolution of emotional conflicts.

Menopause. A physician may recommend medical treatments for women with *low circulating hormones*. Osphena is a non-estrogen medical alternative that, "works like estrogen in the lining of the uterus." In pill form, it has systemic effects and thus "can work differently in other parts of the body" (www.osphena.com). This product facilitates arousal and diminishes pain in post-menopausal women. An estrogen alternative, Estring is ring shaped device that is placed in the vagina for up to 90 days. VagFem is an estradiol vaginal tablet, that is inserted into the vagina with an applicator and dissolves.

The aforementioned prescriptions for postmenopausal women work to restore the vaginal environment and reduce symptoms of itching, pain, decreased lubrication, burning, and urinary dysfunction. There are side effects and risks associated with the use of any form of medical treatment. They can be as mild as nausea or headache, and as severe as stroke or cancer. In order to make an informed decision regarding your personal care, consult your healthcare professional for a complete description of the risks.

A non-medical treatment – sex, sex, and more sex – can serve as the panacea for problems with desire and arousal. Remember the law of inertia: a body in motion stays in motion. Keep your body moving.

It is important to inundate yourself with sexual material. Using the assortment of implements at your disposal, stimulate your mind and body. Watch movies, read books, have conversations, self-pleasure (regularly). There may be underlying conflicts or past sexual abuse/experiences that interfere with your sexual expression. Talking to a professional may be helpful in resolving these issues.

For further assistance with sexual disorders and dysfunctions, there is a list of recommended books and websites in Appendix F. While there is useful information on the Internet, I caution you against surfing the web for solutions. The Internet has a very diverse pool of input. Some of it may be accurate, however, some information is false. Also, in my practice I have seen individuals use the Internet to obsess about their signs and symptoms, spending hours going from website to website, only to increase fear and anxiety. Seek out facts. Don't fall prey to the overwhelming access to unverified information.

DINNER FOR ONE: SELF INDULGENCE

Mirror Exercises

Too often we ignore the things that are right in front of us. That ends today.

Body image can be a significant deterrent when it comes to feeling comfortable in a sexual situation. Sometimes our expectations are unrealistic. As we age, so does our body. It lives through childbirth, injury, surgery, weight gain and loss. We must take for granted that our genetic make-up will be reflected in our appearance. However, individuals do have some effect on how the body looks and feels. This is dependent upon self-care. If you have nurtured your body, cheers! If you have neglected your body, now is your chance to make a change for the better. Today, commit to being a better caregiver of your self.

INDEPENDENT STUDY.

Stand in front of a mirror. Take as much time as you need. Look, really see yourself. Focus on identifying the unique aspects of your body. Think about how it has served you throughout the years. Has it changed? Are there changes that you wish to make? If so, make them. Eat well and stay active. Look and feel good naked!

You should be able to identify all of your private parts. For those of you who need to become familiar with your genitals, take this opportunity to get a good look. Use a hand held mirror and take your time exploring. Get the information needed to make an introduction to your partner. Hello!

CHEF'S GROCERY LIST

What I Love About My Body

What I Dislike About My Body

What I Would Change About My Body

The Sexiest Part of Me

SOUS CHEF'S GROCERY LIST

What I Love About My Body

What I Dislike About My Body

What I Would Change About My Body

The Sexiest Part of Me

My Reflection

COOKING CLASS ASSIGNMENT.

Now that you have looked at yourself more closely, decide what to share in the kitchen. What does your partner need to know about your body image? Can you share your deepest likes, dislikes, wishes and goals? If you cannot yet share them, how can you begin to share? What elements from the previous page can make their way into your recipe box?

Chef's Recipe for Body Image Sharing

Sous Chef's Recipe for Body Image Sharing

Fend for Yourself

In order to achieve real **intimacy**, individuals must first acknowledge the reality of separateness. Sometimes a person does not feel like sharing and you must fend for yourself. Even in the healthiest relationships, each person has separate and unique feelings, thoughts, boundaries, interests, plans, desires, hopes, hang-ups, and hostilities.

There is a fusion in the beginning of a new romance. It's when people are stuck together like white on rice. This ideal phase is characterized by the *fantasy of perfection.* "I am perfect; you are perfect; and we are perfect for each other." As the *ideal phase* gives way to the *real phase*, and the reality of imperfection is now visible, this closeness must give way to separateness. "I can be me and you can be you; and it is all good."

Despite not being forever in a fused state, the relationship is able to maintain a closeness that allows for mutuality: a mature adult-love relationship where the partners get to reap the benefits of being connected to a whole and separate other. The true individual brings unique experiences and knowledge to the relationship. Thus, making a way for mutual interdependence.

Under the circumstances of healthy separateness, there is more to share. There is also, however, a greater potential for conflict. It is this aspect of separateness–the differences between people–that causes difficulties. Many people deal with conflict as if it were an allergen. Avoid, avoid, avoid. It is my contention that healthy conflict is an invaluable resource when it comes to intimacy. Any effort directed at resolution has the potential to bring people closer. If it is done right, he will learn something about her and she will learn something about him; hopefully they reach a suitable compromise.

Personal Pleasure

Before you begin to focus on how to please each other, it is important that you have a good idea about what whets your appetite. Spend some time exploring your own tastes. Get to know your body, sexual desires, fears, and fantasies. The personal pleasure massage is your time to be selfish, a time free of expectations or spectators. Focus on your own erotic needs and pleasures.

This personal massage, which I call *Sexploration* exercises, will take place in three stages: genital exclusion, genital inclusion without climax, and genital inclusion with climax. The number of sessions required to complete this will vary depending on your interests and level of comfort. Explore for as long as you feel comfortable and repeat as many times as you deem necessary to gather the information you are seeking.

Me, Myself, and I

What's the largest erogenous zone in the human body? The brain. Really. With the right focus, we can generate high levels of arousal. However, to accomplish this a person must be in the appropriate state of mind. Relaxed. Present. It is important to stay in the here-and-now during the initial stages of the personal massage. In the final stage, there will be an opportunity to use fantasy to stimulate yourself to climax, if so desired.

Personal awareness is so important in this next series of exercises. Tune out the world so that you can be focused on yourself. Self-discovery is necessary, it will enable you to communicate what you have learned about your body and how it responds to your partner. You will first communicate with words and then with a hands-on lesson. You have probably heard the saying, "I can show you better than I can tell you." That is exactly what you are preparing to do.

Think about this as making love to yourself. Create an environment that will reflect what you want in a sexual experience. Set the **mood**. **Mood** is a temporary state of mind or feeling; it can be affected by many factors, some internal and others external. The **mood** can be romantic, playful, serious, adventurous, relaxed, or kinky. Remember, have it your way. **Setting**, which includes the external factors that create context, is often essential to creating a **mood**. This includes time, place, and surroundings. Make sure the **setting** corresponds to the **mood** that you seek.

For example, a person who wants to create a relaxing **mood** might first need to clear their plate of responsibility. Handle your business so you can stay in the moment. Your body should be the only thing on your mind. Turn off the phone along with all the bells and whistles that alert you to the responsibilities of the day. Take a long bath. Groom. Perfume. Slip into something sexy. Breathe. Imagine a peaceful place. Get your mind right. Dim the lights. Turn on a sound machine or music that turns you on. Make sure you have everything you need within arm's reach.

I encourage you to think outside of the box. Use a variety of textures to help you identify a variety of sensations. Silk ties, leather belts, cotton T's, terrycloth, wood spoons, vibrators. Use all of them, none of them, and feel free to add to the list. I won't tell you how to use these items. That is totally up to you.

Taste Test

The first stage of personal massage does *not* include genital exploration. Therefore, you may want to leave on your underwear to discourage roaming into these areas prematurely. Our sexuality is much more than our genitals. Sometimes we can get so focused on them that we forget about the rest of the body. Therefore, start *without* genital touching. Genital exploration will be incorporated in the next phase of personal massage.

Once you have finished the first stage of touching, read the next section. It will provide instructions about moving on to touching with genital inclusion without climax, and then, finally, to personal massage with genital inclusion and climax. Each phase will come with time to reflect on what you noticed.

Sexploration 1: Touching, Genital Exclusion

INDEPENDENT STUDY.

Using different touches and tactile sensations, take time to explore your body. Explore from head to toe; however, exclude the genitals. Use "I" statement's to communicate your preferences.

Chef's Notes on Sexploration 1...

I like... _____
_____
_____
_____
_____

I dislike... _____
_____
_____
_____
_____

Sous Chef's Notes on Sexploration 1...

I like... _____
_____
_____
_____
_____

I dislike... _____
_____
_____
_____
_____

Sexploration 2: Inclusion of Genitals, No Climax

INDEPENDENT STUDY.

The next series of touches will include the genitals. However, the initial objective is *not* arousal. Use light caresses to explore the genitals; feel free to use the accessories mentioned in the previous section to gather information about various sensations. If you find yourself getting excited, take note of the various sensations that signify arousal.

Chef's Notes on Sexploration 2...

I like... _____

_____

_____

_____

_____

I dislike... _____

_____

_____

_____

_____

Sous Chef's Notes on Sexploration 2...

I like... _____

_____

_____

_____

_____

I dislike... _____

_____

_____

_____

_____

Sexploration 3: Inclusion of Genitals, with Climax

INDEPENDENT STUDY.

This last series of touches will include the genitals and you can explore your body until you reach climax, if desired. In this stage of Sexploration, be mindful of the various physiological and subjective feelings that accompany each stage of arousal (excitement, plateau, orgasm, resolution).

After you have successfully completed the personal massage and noted the outcome, feel free to use fantasy and sex toys as a means of arousal. It is difficult to focus on more than one thing at a time. So, be sure to distinguish between your here-and-now experience and the one that incorporates fantasy and accessories.

I must emphasize the importance of being relaxed. It's hard to get turned on when you are stressed out! This woman used the **setting** to help her relax as she generated a great deal of pleasure.

> "I actually got into the bathtub and opened my legs and ran medium to high running water in between my legs."

Chef's Notes on Sexploration 3...

I like... _____

_____

_____

I dislike... _____

_____

_____

Sous Chef's Notes on Sexploration 3...

I like... _____

_____

_____

I dislike... _____

_____

_____

Keep the Chef Happy

INDEPENDENT STUDY.

Create a narrative focusing on the various sensations that you experienced as you explored your body. Be mindful of touches that make you uncomfortable, as well as those that excite you. The ingredients that we use in our recipe are unique to our own personal desires and dislikes. Use "I" statements to communicate this information to your partner. For example, "I like gentle touches," " I wish we could take more time with caressing," "I will tell you when you hit the right spot."

Chef's Notes on Sensations Experienced During Exploration...

_____
_____
_____
_____
_____
_____
_____
_____
_____

Sous Chef's Notes on Sensations Experienced During Exploration...

_____
_____
_____
_____
_____
_____
_____
_____
_____

My Secret Recipe
INDEPENDENT STUDY.

Building on the work you have just completed, think about what gives you the most pleasure, in and out of the bedroom. Consider your entire relationship. It may be that you love his sense of humor or her spontaneity. List these items – the *ingredients for pleasure* – in your own personal *recipe for ecstasy*. Stay mindful that you are creating a list of things that will eventually be used by your partner to please you. For example, "I like when we take the time to set the mood", "I like it when you wear boxers and smell good", "I like it when we make love with the lights on." or "I like it when we have date night a least once a month."

Chef's Recipe for Pleasure

Sous Chef's Recipe for Pleasure

The Secret Ingredient (Kegel Exercises)

Everyone (men and women) should Kegel to promote sexual health. These exercises isolate and work the pubococcygeus muscle (PC muscle) by squeezing and releasing it. The PC muscle can be found by stopping urine in mid-stream. The exercises, however, are done on an empty bladder. They should be done in sets of 3 or 4, 10 to 15 repetitions at a time. There are several variations of Kegel exercises including rapid contractions, slow contractions, and holding the contraction for 3 seconds. The technique may vary, but the objective remains the same: muscle strengthening. Just as when exercising any other muscle, this exercise increases blood flow and improves sexual responsiveness, including greater sexual control, stronger erections and more powerful orgasms!

I recommend scheduling your Kegels around a particular task that you do everyday to help remember them, such as driving to and from work, in the shower, while brushing your teeth. For the tech savvy individual, setting an alert on your Smartphone may be the answer.

There are also several devices for women that may improve the accuracy of the exercise and/or do the work for you. These devices vary in cost and include: automatic pelvic floor exerciser, vaginal weights, and pleasure beads. These tools are available online.

If you doubt the impact of good sexual health, take a look at this man's description of pleasure that resulted from a woman's Kegel workout. He also identified **newness**, **nature of the relationship**, and **love** as key ingredients.

> *"It was 1989 and I was in a relationship with a girl I met when I was living in Chicago. She was a German au pair. I was 27 and she was 21. It was the first or second time we had sex. After the act was over, I did not feel like leaving so I could take a shower. I just wanted to hold her and bask in the afterglow. I felt very close to her and thought it was love. The sex was amazing. She had very developed Kegel muscles due to the fact that she did competitive horse riding."*

INDEPENDENT STUDY.

Identify the best times and places to do your Kegel Exercises. Create a list to help serve as a reminder.

CHEF'S KEGEL CHART		
DAY	TIME	LOCATION

SOUS CHEF'S KEGEL CHART		
DAY	TIME	LOCATION

Part Three: Blending Recipes

DINNER FOR TWO: BUFFET STYLE

Mutual Pleasure

According to Masters and Johnson (1974) "mutual pleasure sets a seal on commitment." They write (p. 254),

> Each partner, to protect his or her own happiness, tries to sustain the other partner's happiness so that their relationship will flourish; and these reciprocal efforts intensify the satisfaction they find in living together – which further strengthens their wish to remain a couple. They live according the commitment of mutual concern, and pleasure is the bond between them.

It is important to understand the role of pleasure in relationships, as well as the impact of its absence. For this reason, couples should never go long periods of time (over two weeks) without mutual pleasure. This may not always come in the form of sexual intercourse. However, healthy sexual expression is a significant part of a successful relationship.

This next series of sexual explorations will involve both partners. Each person will have a chance to be the giver and receiver in every activity. This is an opportunity to share what you have learned, with words and actions. The sequence of touches will resemble the personal massage, starting with (1) no genital touching; moving to (2) genital exploration without climax; and finally (3) genital exploration with climax. During this time, each person will have the opportunity to be the giver and receiver of touches. With the objective of educating your partner about your likes and dislikes, the receiver will use words, and then hands, to guide the giver.

As before, you are encouraged to create a **mood** and **setting** for optimal relaxation and relating. Bathe each other or skip ahead to page **116** and "Put Something New on the Menu." Experiment with various tactile sensations (e.g. silk, cotton, leather, terrycloth); feel free to incorporate the other senses. This massage can be as playful or as sensual as you make it. While many people use oils and lotions for massage, there may be other ingredients that get the job done, too. Honey. Chocolate syrup. Whipped cream.

The following narratives may inspire you. In the first narrative, take note of how the **mood** was set, as they expressed their **mutual love** and **passion**.

> *"The most sexually satisfying experience of my life is when my wife was freshly showered, sporting a nighty, and smelling as fresh as a rose. We rubbed each other down with body oils while soft music played in the background. We engaged in deep kissing and touching as we confessed our love for each other before we had intercourse."*

> *"Being with a guy who mentally and physically stimulated me; he was able to keep up with me sexually as far as my appetite and stamina and was not afraid to explore my body and I, his."*

> *"When my spouse fondled my prostate."*

WORKING TOGETHER IN THE KITCHEN

Mutual pleasure work is to be spread over the course of a week or two. Decide who will be the giver and the receiver. Remember there will be three stages to this *sexploration* and you each get a turn in each role. That adds up to a minimum of six experiences of giving and receiving pleasure. Six!

Sexploration 1: Touching, Genital Exclusion

During the first series of touches, the genitals are off limits.

As the *giver*, your job is to apply a variety of touches to your partner. Brush, caress, knead, stroke. Vary the pressure and pace to explore your partner's body. Once you have exhausted the possibilities with your hands, be adventurous – use all different body parts (yours and your partner's). Kiss. Blow. Suck. After completing a vanilla sexploration, you may add variety by incorporating other tactile sensations, as you did in your own personal massage.

As the *receiver*, stay focused on the touches you are experiencing. Make a mental note of what feels good, uncomfortable, or exciting. Can you stay in the moment or does your mind wander? Unless something feels uncomfortable or painful, wait until the end of the exercise to give feedback.

After five or ten minutes switch roles. Remember hands off the genitals. Take your time exploring each other and keep the expectations out of the room for now.

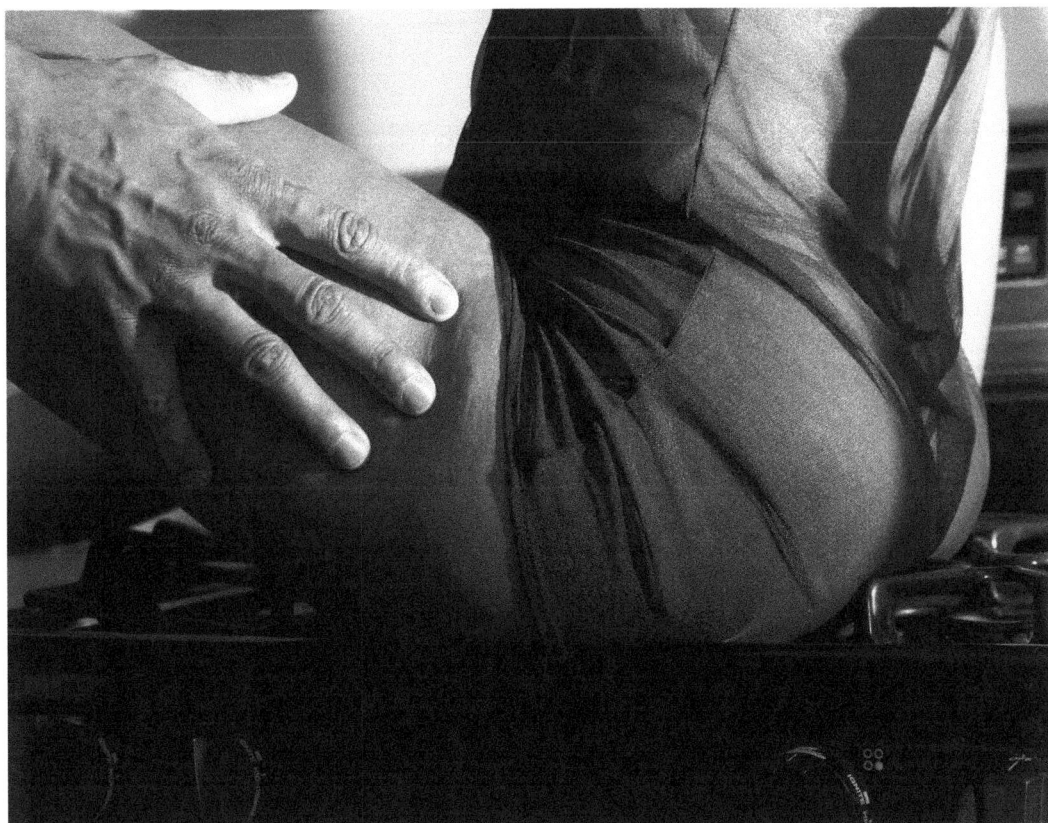

Each person should have an opportunity to be the giver and receiver at least once before moving on to the next stage. If there is any discomfort, repeat this activity before moving on. If sexual arousal occurs you can choose to do nothing or, at the end of the mutual massage, you can give yourself a personal massage. Consider allowing your partner to observe as you self-pleasure; this can be a great source of information and arousal. There should be no pressure to satisfy each other's needs. Feed yourself!

COOKING CLASS ASSIGNMENT.

Reflect on your experience in each role – giver and receiver. Create a narrative focusing on the various sensations that you experienced as you explored each other's bodies. Be mindful of touches that make you uncomfortable, as well as those that excite you. The ingredients that we use in our recipe are unique to our own personal desires and dislikes.

Chef's Notes on Sexploration 1...

I like... _____

_____

_____

I dislike... _____

_____

_____

Sous Chef's Notes on Sexploration 1...

I like... _____

_____

_____

I dislike... _____

_____

_____

Sexploration 2: Touching, Genital Inclusion without Climax

COOKING CLASS ASSIGNMENT.

During the next series of touching exercises, light genital caressing is permitted. Again, the objective is for the receiver to focus on the sensations felt and to communicate this experience to the giver once they have finished. If you want to communicate during the exercise, use only hand-guided instruction.

While sexual arousal is not the objective, it may be the outcome. It is left to your discretion to decide how to relieve the sexual tension that may develop between you. You could do nothing. Live through the experience and talk about it. Or you may decide to engage in *parallel play* (where you self-pleasure along side each other) or mutual masturbation (where you self-pleasure for each other and/or stimulate each other); oral sex is also an option. Remember to have it your way!

Chef's Notes on Sexploration 2...

I like... _____

_____

_____

I dislike... _____

_____

_____

_____

Sous Chef's Notes on Sexploration 2...

I like... _____

_____

_____

I dislike... _____

_____

_____

_____

Sexploration 3: Touching, Genital Inclusion with Climax

Sensual touching can awaken a person's desire. Take the time to set the **mood**, focus on **intimacy**, and shift away from expectations and the goal of climax. This may yield an even more fulfilling experience.

This person did not need to experience an orgasm to feel sexually satisfied. **Passion** and **intimacy** were the only ingredients needed.

> *"My most sexually satisfying experience is when I feel complete with my partner. That's when I feel satisfied sexually … and oddly enough it wasn't each occurrence that an orgasm was met for me, but it was the mental stimulation and the workout [the energy and connection] that made it great."*

Read the next narrative with **mutual pleasure** and **intimacy** in mind. This couple set a **romantic mood, communicated** their desires, and used a **variety** of **accessories** to create an **orgasmic** experience. As with any good meal, **timing** was crucial.

> *"My spouse and I took the whole evening to explore each other and be together. We had low lighting and soft music and did not rush to complete intercourse, but instead removed our clothes and lay and talked and touched and explored, not only with our hands, but with various other tactile experiences: foods, various materials, lotions, etc. When, after a long period of foreplay, we moved on to intercourse, it, too, was slow and interspersed with explorations of positions, talking and taking time to "feel." It was enjoyable because we took the time to feel what our bodies were experiencing, as well as to listen and learn what the other was experiencing. It was not just orgasm with our bodies; our minds were involved as well."*

This couple used massage as foreplay, and carved out a path straight to pleasure.

> *"It started out as a full body massage, then slow kissing, then to all out sexual intercourse."*

COOKING CLASS ASSIGNMENT.

Now you get to have your cake and eat it too. In this final stage of mutual massage with genital exploration, orgasm is permitted – but it is not the goal. You are still gathering information about giving and receiving touches. Have fun as you allow your excitement to build to peak pleasure.

Chef's Notes on Sexploration 3...

I like... _____

_____

_____

_____

I dislike... _____

_____

_____

_____

Sous Chef's Notes on Sexploration 3...

I like... _____

_____

_____

_____

I dislike... _____

_____

_____

_____

Erotic Fusion: Making Your Couple's Recipe

COOKING CLASS ASSIGNMENT.

Review your individual notes and share them with your partner to create your couple's *recipe for ecstasy*. This is your opportunity to show each other how you want to be loved. Both of your tastes should be represented in the following narrative.

Chef's Recipe for How I Want to be Loved

Sous Chef's Recipe for How I Want to be Loved

Set Thyself Aside

A generous lover is a satisfied lover: one who gives without the expectation of reciprocity, yet at the same time guarantees it.

> Generosity, in this context, is a sensitive, feeling response to another person's wants and needs. Acts of generosity and altruism that are an outgrowth of a partner's understanding of the other's uniqueness are the most appreciated by the recipient and bring the most satisfaction to the giver (Firestone, Firestone & Catlett, 2006, p. 265).

> Essentially, there are three aspects of a healthy response to a generous act on the part of one's mate. The first involves being open to accepting what is offered, allowing the other to meet one's needs; the second involves verbally expressing appreciation; and the third entails reciprocal actions – offering generosity and kindness in return (Firestone et al, 2006, p. 265).

This is not a tit-for-tat dynamic. The receiver will instead give to their mate something of value that is a reflection of gained understanding, emanating from the process of sharing one's personal preferences, hopes, dreams, desires, and needs. Simply put, "I understand you and your wish is my command." Seduce him. Undress her.

Read carefully as these narratives provide examples of his **focus on her** and **mutuality**. These men keep their recipes short but sweet!

> "Making intimate love to my wife, morning, afternoon and evening, out of passion and mutual desire."

> "Holed up in a hotel room for a weekend with [a woman who] would become my wife. There were no false pretenses, no games, we loved one another in the way that exciting young couples do … passionately, wildly & completely."

> "When I first started dating this young lady I was in love with around 2005/2006. We seemed to be in tune with each other and our needs; and sex was great."

Women, on the other hand, illuminate their experience with words, and take the recipe from short and sweet to special and spectacular!

For this woman, **timing** and a splash of **passion** added to her sexual pleasure.

> "The most sexually satisfying experience was with a mate that took time to satisfy my whole body. He took his time to see what turned me on and paid close attention to the way my body responded and my reactions to the things he did. The experience lasted over 3 hours and it was memorable and full of passion and pleasure."

This woman spared no expense as her recipe also incorporated **variety in the sex act**, **passion**, and **multiple orgasms**!

> "My most satisfying experience occurred approximately one month ago. My boyfriend and I were giving each other back rubs on the living room

carpet. We turned the satellite channel to "New Age CD" and slowly began to give each other back rubs. After he rubbed my back for approximately 15 minutes, he told me to just relax and enjoy the music. He started to rub my leg down by the calf and he slowly worked his way up my thigh. He continued to tease me for about 10 minutes. He then flipped my body over and began to perform oral sex on me. I reached my first orgasm in about three minutes. He then began kissing me (which in itself makes me so horny). I worked my way down to his penis and performed oral sex on him. We then began to have intercourse in a number of different positions. I know I had at least three more orgasms. Our final position (which is my favorite) was when I was on my knees and he entered me from behind while holding my hips. He reached orgasm and exploded inside me. It was great!"

COOKING CLASS ASSIGNMENT.

Now that you have read some examples, it is your turn to put someone else's needs first. To this end, the next exercise will accentuate the differences between partners. Once you have identified those differences, list them, and use the list to create moments where you get to focus on the needs of the other person. This is a time where you will give altruistically to your partner without the expectation of reciprocity. Instead, gratification will come from your partner's pleasure. Don't just focus on the bedroom – think about your entire relationship.

That's right! Set thyself aside and focus on the other.

CHEF'S GROCERY LIST
My Preferences

SOUS CHEF'S GROCERY LIST
My Preferences

Chef's Recipe for Pleasing My Partner

Sous Chef's Recipe for Pleasing My Partner

MENU PLANNING

Check Your Temperature

It's time to learn more about yourself. Are you ready? Use your smart phone, journal, "reminder," sticky note, the form provided, or whatever helps you to keep track of your life to identify the times that you are feeling frisky, hungry, horny, or amorous. Use this information to complete the next task: Sex is on the menu.

INDEPENDENT STUDY.

Take a week or two and record at different times of day whether you felt hot, medium, or cold. *Hot* means that you were ready and actively thinking about a sexual encounter and/or you experienced physical signs of arousal, including an erection or tingling genitals. *Medium* means that you had fleeting thoughts of sex that were not accompanied by signs of arousal. You were not quite ready, but a slight increase in temperature encouraged by a sexual stimulus would put you in the ***mood***. *Cold* means that sex was not on the menu. There was a complete absence of sexual thoughts and feelings.

Check your temperature. Are you cold, medium, or hot?

Chef's Temperature Chart

	Breakfast	Lunch	Dinner	Midnight Snack
Sun				
Mon				
Tue				
Wed				
Thu				
Fri				
Sat				
Sun				
Mon				
Tue				
Wed				
Thu				
Fri				
Sat				

Sous Chef's Temperature Chart

	Breakfast	Lunch	Dinner	Midnight Snack
Sun				
Mon				
Tue				
Wed				
Thu				
Fri				
Sat				
Sun				
Mon				
Tue				
Wed				
Thu				
Fri				
Sat				

Make Reservations

Schedule it! Have a culinary planning meeting between Chef and Sous Chef. Bring your temperature charts. Learn about each other – see what times of day find you both in the hot or medium temperature range. Notice if one of you is hot when the other is repeatedly cold. Learn about each other and think about how you can make the most of the times when you are both in – or close to in – the **mood**.

Now that you have identified the ideal time to have sex, put it on the menu. Spontaneity is important; however, sometimes life gets too busy to allow time for all of the things that we enjoy. One way to optimize your time is to schedule it. It is important to know when both partners are available and when you both are hot and ready.

It is rare that both people will consistently desire sex at the same time. Expect there to be conflicts in frequency of interests, as well as timing. *The goal is not to get you in sync, but to create realistic expectations for pleasurable moments together.* On the days that sex is not a realistic option, substitutions are allowed. Spend **intentional time** and create **meaningful moments**. Remember that every lovemaking session will not be a full course meal. Put a "quickie" on the menu. It is important to understand that scheduled time together does not mean monotony or boredom. Even when sex is planned, you can still create fun and exciting ways to get started. Mix it up!

For this married woman, sexual satisfaction was linked to a **time** when her schedule was clear of the duties associated with motherhood.

> *"The first few years with my husband. We are very good together and at that point had few responsibilities (and no kids) so we could be spontaneous and not have to worry about anything. We would spend entire weekends doing nothing but enjoying each other."*

Sex is on the Menu

COOKING CLASS ASSIGNMENT.

Now that you have collaborated with your partner, pick a few ideal times to have sex. Stick to it!

COUPLE'S IDEAL TIMES TO HAVE SEX			
	BREAKFAST	LUNCH	DINNER	MIDNIGHT SNACK
SUN				
MON				
TUE				
WED				
THU				
FRI				
SAT				

TURN ON THE HEAT

Now that you have sorted out *what* you each like and *when* you each like to do it, now you get to work on your sexual richness as a couple. You know how and when to get into the groove – you're going to deepen the groove, together.

Whet the Palate

The following narratives provide examples of the different phases of the sexual response cycle: excitement (arousal), plateau, orgasm, and resolution. (see p. 12)

In the first narrative the woman identifies **setting** ("at the hotel" and "in the jacuzzi") and **mood** as being instrumental to **arousal**. Fondling increased her level of **arousal**. She identifies the plateau phase as "before orgasm" and "continued lovemaking" until climax.

> *"My most satisfying experience involved an ex-boyfriend, J. We went to a hotel with a Jacuzzi in the room. After arriving, getting settled and eating dinner, we sat in the Jacuzzi, naked. He began to fondle my breasts and vagina. He sat me on top of the side of the Jacuzzi and toyed with my vagina. At that point, we began to make love in the Jacuzzi. Before orgasm, we got into the bed and continued the lovemaking until both of us orgasmed."*

Anticipation builds in the next narrative, as the lovers have been disconnected for some time. This recipe includes many ingredients of the *recipe for ecstasy* including **nature of the relationship**, **setting**, **engendered feelings**, and **communication**. The **technique** is slow and intentional in the arousal phase. There is "tension" in the plateau phase, and you can just about guess what happened next. Orgasm!!

> *"It was with a reunited love from long ago. We met in a beautiful hotel and spent the first moments reconnecting (nervous and anxious about the act about to happen). He rubbed my feet while we talked, I rubbed his hair and chest as he laid across my lap and then he asked if he could kiss me … WOW! We kissed and as the tension built I told him that I wanted him to make love to me NOW! We did and it was just as amazing as we thought it would be. He was strong and confident and took me to places I hadn't been. We made love several times that day (which at our age I thought was impossible for men to do!). We couldn't keep our hands off of one another and before he left, he grabbed me and made love to me one last time and as he held my legs apart he looked down at me and said, "Who's is it?" To which I replied without hesitation, "Baby, IT"S YOURS!!!" Amazing!"*

Fake It Until You Make It

This is the only time where faking an orgasm is an acceptable practice. If you have faked an orgasm in the past to "get it over with," to appease your partner, or to avoid dealing with the reality of sexual dysfunction, you are depriving you and your partner of pleasure. A person can't improve or attend to your needs if they are unaware. Faking an orgasm is a source of deception and only creates distance between partners. The lying stops here.

With that preface in mind, *simulating* the orgasmic experience can facilitate the process of learning to let go. If reaching an orgasm is difficult, experts recommend that you fake it until you make it. I'm not talking about deceiving yourself or partner. Use a technique called *plateauing* to simulate the experience of orgasm. Self-pleasure; when you reach the plateau stage contract the PC muscle, increase your breathing, flail, moan, scream and gyrate. This is done in an effort to train you to have an orgasmic response.

Moan... Sigh... SCREAM!

Keep it Cumming

This next recipe includes plenty of foreplay and the ingredients **newness** and **mood** (*anticipation*), which facilitated **arousal**. The temperature got so hot that she was able to experience a vaginal **orgasm** for the first time.

> "The first time with my current partner. We engaged in a lot of foreplay that actually started the night before. We spent a lot of time kissing and touching but we didn't actually have sex then. The next night we continued the foreplay and then we had intercourse. I had an orgasm from vaginal penetration during our sex before he climaxed which is rare for me. Then continued until he climaxed. It was great. I've never had anyone bring me to climax vaginally the first time we had sex."

This woman uses the power of connection to motivate her partner to give her **multiple orgasms**.

> "I went to her house and she was laying in the bed and she told me, 'I have something to tell [you]. The more orgasms [you] give me, the more connected to the great energy source we will be come.' We had sex for 3 days straight. I came so many times I lost count."

Live through the frustration and before you know it you will be enjoying powerful **orgasms**. Who wouldn't want to experience this? It is worth working on it.

"Ball of excitement from deep within rising gradually from the tip of my toes and fingers and drawing in closer to my center, then exploding in a wave of great sensation spreading throughout my body. It felt like energy contained and released at the same time."

OHYES! OHNO! OHSHIT!

Ooo-wee!

Mmmm hmmm

Big Daddy

Please...

Jesus!

There is no limit to the myriad of expressions to alert you that your dish is done.

DING!

The Taste of Pleasure

While it is believed that the male and female subjective experience of orgasm is similar, we all have a unique way of expressing peak pleasure.

INDEPENDENT STUDY.

Describe your orgasm to your partner in the most vivid way possible. Find adjectives, metaphors, and images that bring the orgasmic experience to life.

For example:

- My orgasm feels like a doorbell ringing ... ding-dong.
- My orgasm feels like a finale at the fireworks.
- My orgasm feels like a like a volcano erupting.
- My orgasm feels fantastic.

Chef's Notes on What My Orgasms Feel Like...

Sous Chef's Notes on What My Orgasms Feel Like...

FINALLY! COOKING IT UP TOGETHER

Your Daily Diet (Recommended Daily Allowance)

All relationships have their routines, even in the bedroom. Routines can be very valuable. They promote structure, consistency, and security. Think about your daily interactions. Has the intimacy between you become stale? Sometimes it is important to break the monotony. Infuse the relationship with spontaneity and fun. This man did not have one particular experience to share, however, he emphasized the importance of **newness** and unpredictability.

> *"[I] can't say there was [one] experience, I have generally enjoyed most of the experiences. something new is usually the biggest turn on; new partner, new experience, new location."*

Follow his recipe; step outside of your comfort zone and allow growth to take place. Start with the staple items – the ingredients that are always on the menu. The same positions, sequence of events, room in the house, conversations, TV shows, dinner plans, arguments, habits, and relational patterns. Then think of how you would like to mix it up. Allow yourself to indulge your wildest fantasy. These fantasies should not just revolve around the bedroom. What would fulfill your dreams? Sex in the rain, a nice vacation, a nightly stroll hand-in-hand, more kissing.

Here is a routine that generated a great deal of pleasure. Maybe it's the simplicity of it.

> *"[A] weekend day where we woke up, had sex, ate, slept, had more sex. Wash, rinse, repeat."*

Another bite of this dish, however, reveals the nuances of this *recipe for ecstasy*. A pinch of **sexual abandon** allowed them to escape the monotony. **Variety** and **intimacy** was added to taste. This couple created an experience of **awayness** without leaving the room. They got lost in each other. Using their senses to guide the way, they found ecstasy.

> *"We were both into one another. I have a very sensitive nose and her body scent is irresistible. She was willing to try new positions and techniques, including things that were "taboo." Our bodies naturally mesh with one another. Her breath smelled good even though it was the first thing in the morning. Her pussy tasted good and smelled wonderful. We talked during. We kissed. We watched porn. We played with toys. We heard our phones and ignored them. We made noise despite who may have cared."*

Spice up Your Pantry: Sexual Fantasies

In this activity you will co-create a *recipe for ecstasy*. If you could have your heart's desire, without fear of judgment, without concern regarding performance, with no expectations too high, no desire too unbecoming – if you could have all of this, what would excite you the most? Remove any and all inhibitions. Forget about the taboo. Let your mind go; abandon yourself to sexual pleasure.

Need inspiration? One person noted that their most sexually satisfying experience was, *"When we have sex and I've been allowed to explore more of my fantasies without any hesitation from my partner."* It can be as kinky or as innocent as you want. It is not always about acting out or role-play.

Having a mental script to bring to mind during the sexual act might also spark excitement. It may be just what you need to turn your everyday-ordinary into special-occasion-extraordinary. See Appendix F for recommendations on adding variety and spice.

INDEPENDENT STUDY.

List the special ingredients needed to make your dreams a reality. This may include accessories such as soft music, personal lubricant, and handcuffs. A wall mirror might also come in handy. Close your eyes. Picture your most erotic dream. Write down what comes to mind.

CHEF'S
GROCERY LIST

My Specialty Ingredients for

Fantasy

SOUS CHEF'S
GROCERY LIST

My Specialty Ingredients for

Fantasy

Now, create a narrative with your specialty ingredients. Picture where your partner will fit in.

Chef's Recipe for Sexual Fantasy

Sous Chef's Recipe for Sexual Fantasy

Fantasy Pantry

COOKING CLASS ASSIGNMENT.

Time for a kitchen planning meeting! Compare your notes. Are you surprised with your partner's fantasies? Do your fantasies match? Together, complete one or more Sexual Fantasy Recipe Cards.

Couple's Recipe for Sexual Fantasy

Couple's Recipe for Sexual Fantasy

Role-Play

Have sex with a stranger. In this case, the stranger is your partner and you are role-playing to add a little spice to your sex life. Take this narrative that includes **variety** and **mutuality** for example:

> "When we role-play and have edibles and oils. When we explore each other's bodies to see what makes us get off. One the hottest times was when we rented a motel, watched X-rated movies and fucked in front of a mirror for hours. We took each other there. I played a prostitute and he was my john. I even got paid at the end. LOL."

INDEPENDENT STUDY.

Role-playing is sometimes an aspect of fantasy. Think about some roles that might excite you. Allow your imagination to run wild and create scenarios that you and your partner can act-out.

Chef's Notes on Role-Playing Scenarios...

_____
_____
_____
_____
_____
_____

SousChef's Notes on Role-Playing Scenarios...

_____
_____
_____
_____
_____
_____
_____

COOKING CLASS ASSIGNMENT.

Now collaborate with your partner and decide on the scenarios you want to act-out. It is important that you are both comfortable with role-play. Therefore, only agree to roles that will result in mutual pleasure.

Couple's Recipe for Role-Play

Couple's Recipe for Role-Play

Feast

Individuals who have trouble with sexual interest or desire may need some help stimulating their appetites. Inundate yourself with erotic material including books, videos, magazines, music, and movies. Choose things that you think will arouse you, but at the same time try something new, order from off the menu. For those of you who don't have any trouble with your sexual appetite, use the following narratives to better understand the role of being playful and spicing things up. A good measure of "good-enough sex" is the occasional presence of playfulness. This may be because for play to occur, other aspects of intimacy must be functioning well: trust, mutual acceptance, priority of pleasure, freedom to be oneself, and deep valuing of the relationship [Metz & McCarthy, 2007].

Variety is the Spice of Life

Variety can be as simple as, *"I was blindfolded and stimulated in many different ways by my partner,"* or as elaborate as the narratives that follow. It's the kind of recipe that might take all day and night.

Variation in the sex act, for this man, included accessories, role-play, **sexual abandon**, and sexual position.

> *"I had a friend come to work with me. She said she wanted to do something freaky with me so I took her to a garage at a closed facility in our city. She said she wanted to be handcuffed and treated rough. I handcuffed her behind her back and played like she was under arrest. I then bent her over the trunk of the car and had sex with her from behind until I had an orgasm. What made it so exciting? The excitement [and the fact that it was on the job and outside]."*

In the next narrative there are several components to the sexual experience, including role-play, **sexual abandon**, **arousal**, **setting**, **timing**, and accessories. But the most salient feature of her erotic experience was the **variety**.

> *"The most sexually satisfying experience was with a friend that I have who is willing to do any and everything I am willing to do and more. No holding back and the sky is the limit with positions, toys, romance, locations, role playing, time of day."*

Some people take a little pain with their pleasure.

> *"I would have to say that all of them are generally great. However, anal sex has been a work in progress. So, the first time that she was able to give it up with out being uncomfortable or in any pain and actually enjoyed the penetration doggy style, the orgasms that we both had were incredible."*

Or a little fear and titillation inspired by the unknown.

> *"I had gone over to my partner's house. He decided to try something different, so he blindfolded me and laid me on the bed. He spread my legs and began to shave/trim the hair in my vaginal area. After he cleaned off*

the shaving cream, he began to lick my private area until I had an orgasm. Then he took a vibrator and moved it in all the right ways and I reached an orgasm again. He took off the blindfold and held me upside down while he fucked me to my third orgasm."

Going Rogue in the Kitchen

Changing sexual positions is an easy way to add **variety** to your sex life. Different positions can also help reduce sexual dysfunction, pain or discomfort that are associated with aging or certain medical conditions. Experiment with the many ways to give each other pleasure by challenging your body to stretch, bend, bounce, roll.

Certain positions such as the *cowgirl* (woman on top) give a woman greater control over the parts of the vagina that are stimulated, as well as control over the pace. He gets a full view of her plump breasts and has his hands free to roam all over her body. *Doggy style* gives a male the opportunity for deep penetration. Now he is in control. Banging her with the force he desires, looking at her voluptuous backside, and if he wants to get a little rough (and she says that it's okay) he can spank that ass or pull her hair. Couples can tweak a recipe with a slight substitution, and *voila!* From "doggy style" to "lazy dog" or "cowgirl" to "reverse cowgirl." If you are really feeling adventurous, try Beyonce's (2013) signature move - surfboard. "Fill the tub up half way then ride it with my surfboard." Add this, subtract that, a slight **variation**, and you have created an entirely new, scrumptious, recipe.

Read the following narratives with positions in mind. They also highlight the role of **mood**, **setting**, **variety**, and foreplay in sexual satisfaction. Lots of kissing, sexual talk (**communication**), and **playfulness** increase the level of **anticipation** and **arousal**, culminating in **orgasm**.

"This had been over 7 years ago. We had gone to a hotel and I had bought some lingerie and modeled them off to him. After, I had done all that he asked me to lie on the bed and he started to massage my feet while kissing me on my calf. Once he was done with that he started to lick on my inner thighs. Working his way up to sucking on one of my breasts. Then [he] looked at me and said, "[I] don't want the other one to get jealous. [He began] to suck on my other breast. As he was doing that I was licking in his ear and kissing his neck. Then he just flips me over and starts kissing me on my back, butt and legs. We proceeded to fuck profusely doggy style. With him banging the shit out of my pussy. I had an orgasm then he turned me over and we did it missionary position. While we both were kissing and licking on each other he pressed my hips downward while thrusting himself inside of me. We both had an orgasm. I still think of that day."

Or even better, this experience of **multiple orgasms** that highlights a **romantic mood, intimacy, variety**, positions, **communication**, and **satiety**.

"My partner and I had candles lit and were lying in bed talking and caressing each other. He looked into my eyes and told me how much he loved me, and began kissing me. We became immediately passionate and held tightly, kissing each other. He then went down on me and made me reach orgasm two times. I begged for him to put it inside me. He put himself in my mouth and I sucked it until he came. He stayed hard and began fucking me hard like we both wanted. He rolled me over on my side and entered from behind. He then told me to reach for my vibrator and put it on my clitoris while he fucked me. After I had another orgasm, he told me to reach for the lubricant on the nightstand. He put it all over me, and took me anally. As he stroked gently in and out, we both had orgasms several times. We ended by holding in exhaustion and feeling like we could do anything with each other. We talked about how wonderful it was and held tight for some time."

Cookie Cutters (Sexual Postions)

Sexual positions are like an assortment of flavors. There are so many to choose from, you might just take your time and try a different one each night. Don't be intimidated by some of the outrageous stunts you see in the media (e.g., sex hanging from a shower rod or standing on your head). Stay mindful of your physical capabilities, limitations, and personal desires. Certain positions may prove to minimize pain, optimize pleasure, and provide the necessary ingredients for more powerful orgasms. I have chosen some of my personal favorites to share with you here. The list, however, is far from exhaustive. Therefore, feel free to add to the collection of cookie cutters that has been started.

INDEPENDENT STUDY.

Before you peak at my suggestions, write down the positions that give you the most pleasure. If you don't have experience with different positions, use your imagination, and identify some positions you would like to try.

Chef's Notes on Favorite Positions...

SousChef's Notes on Favorite Positions...

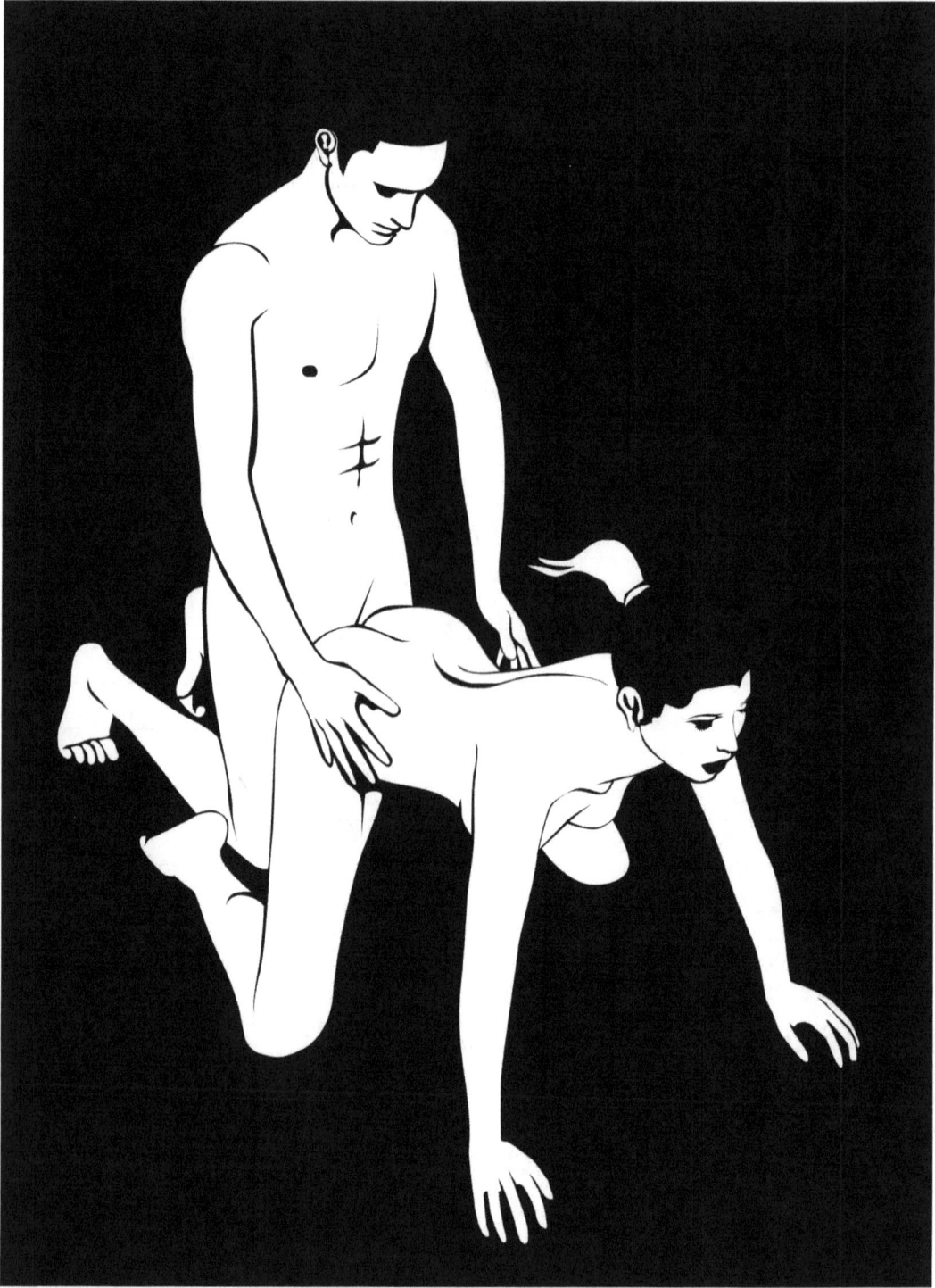

DOGGY STYLE

Entering the partner from the rear, while on all fours.

LAZY DOG

Entering the partner from the rear, while lying on side.

COWGRIL
Female on top, facing partner.

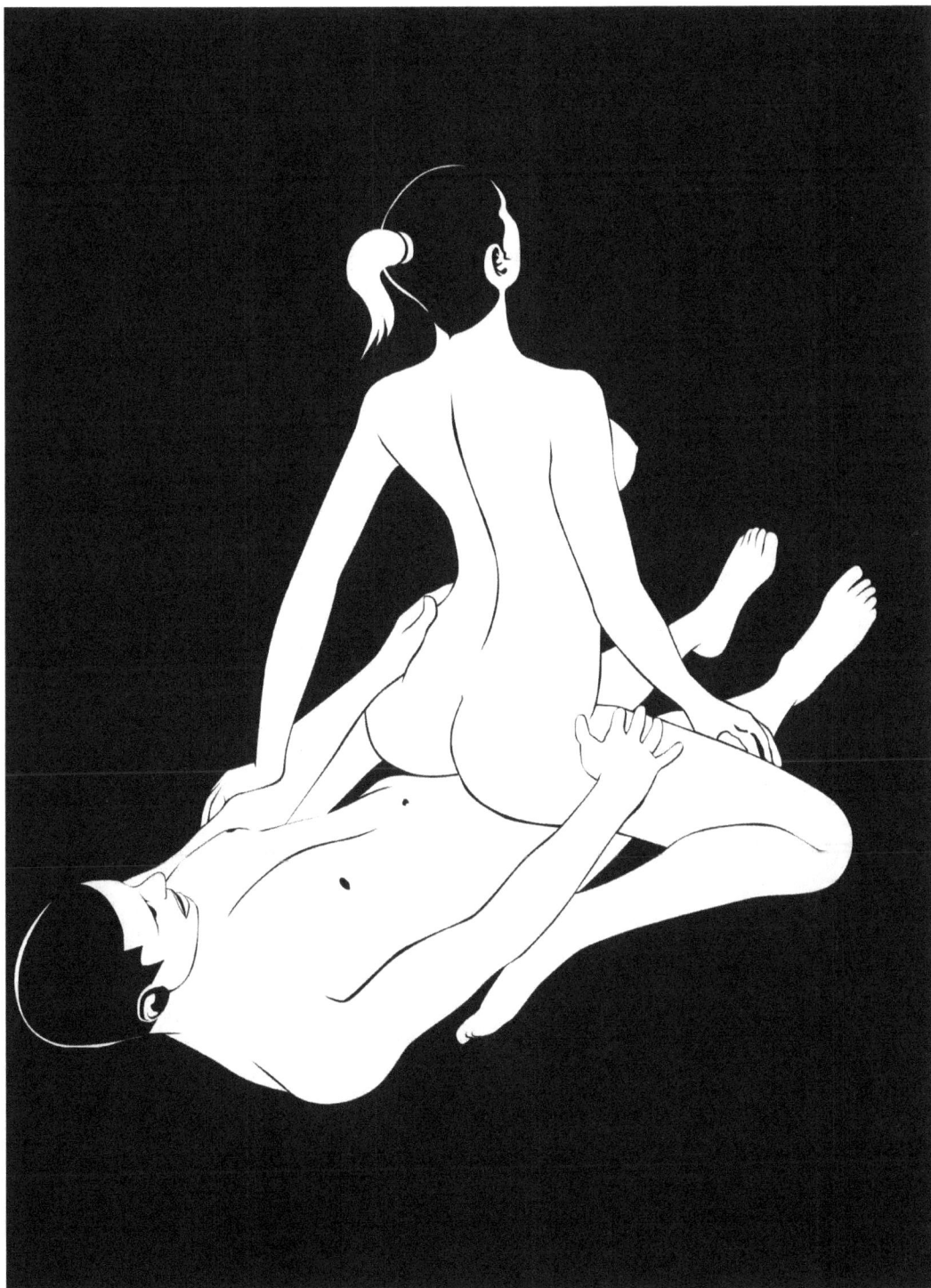

REVERSE COWGIRL
Female on top, while turned away from partner.

STANDING UP

May require the use of a wall for balance, or bending the female partner over a counter.

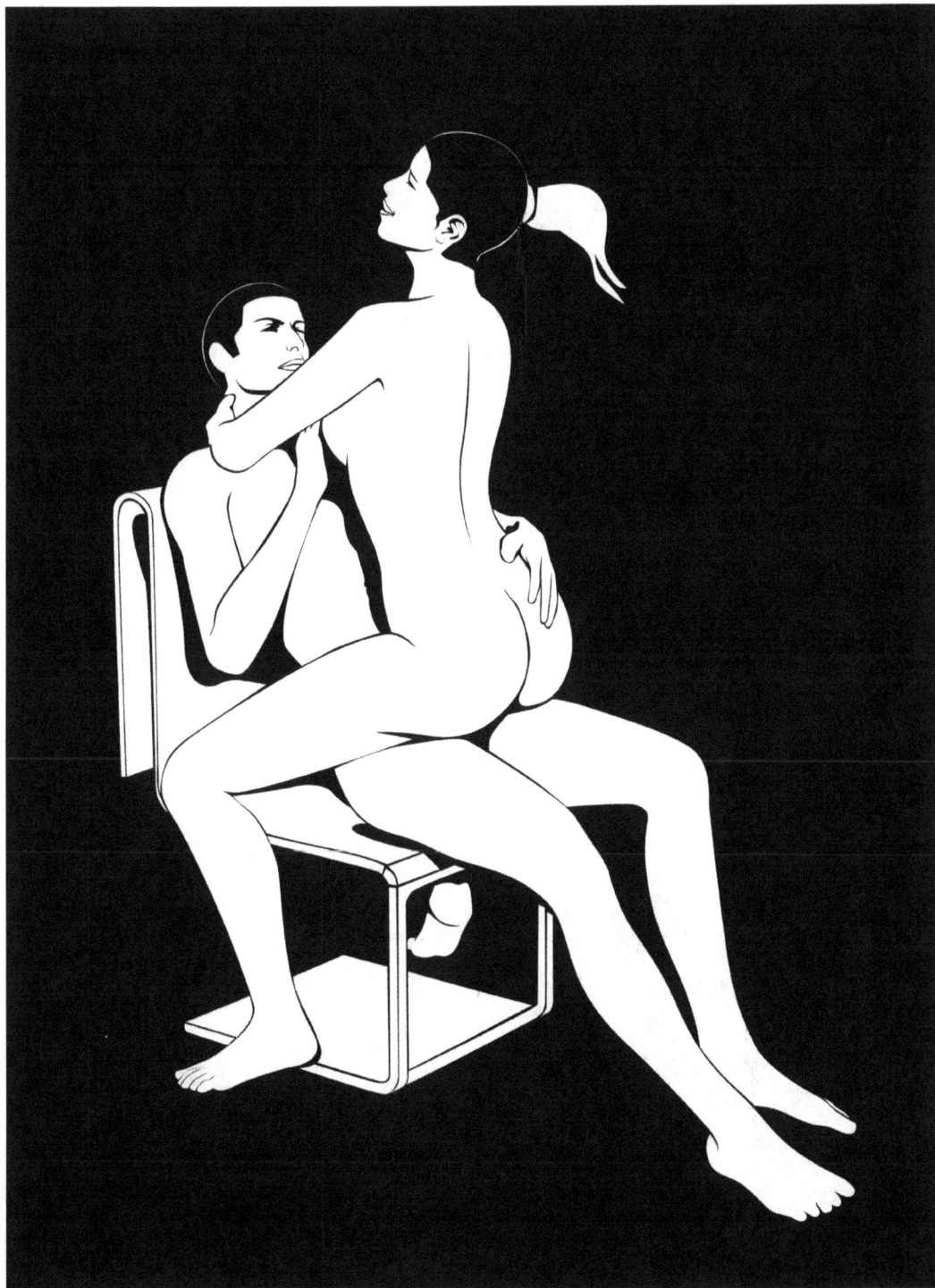

LAP DANCE

Pull up a chair, and have the woman ride.

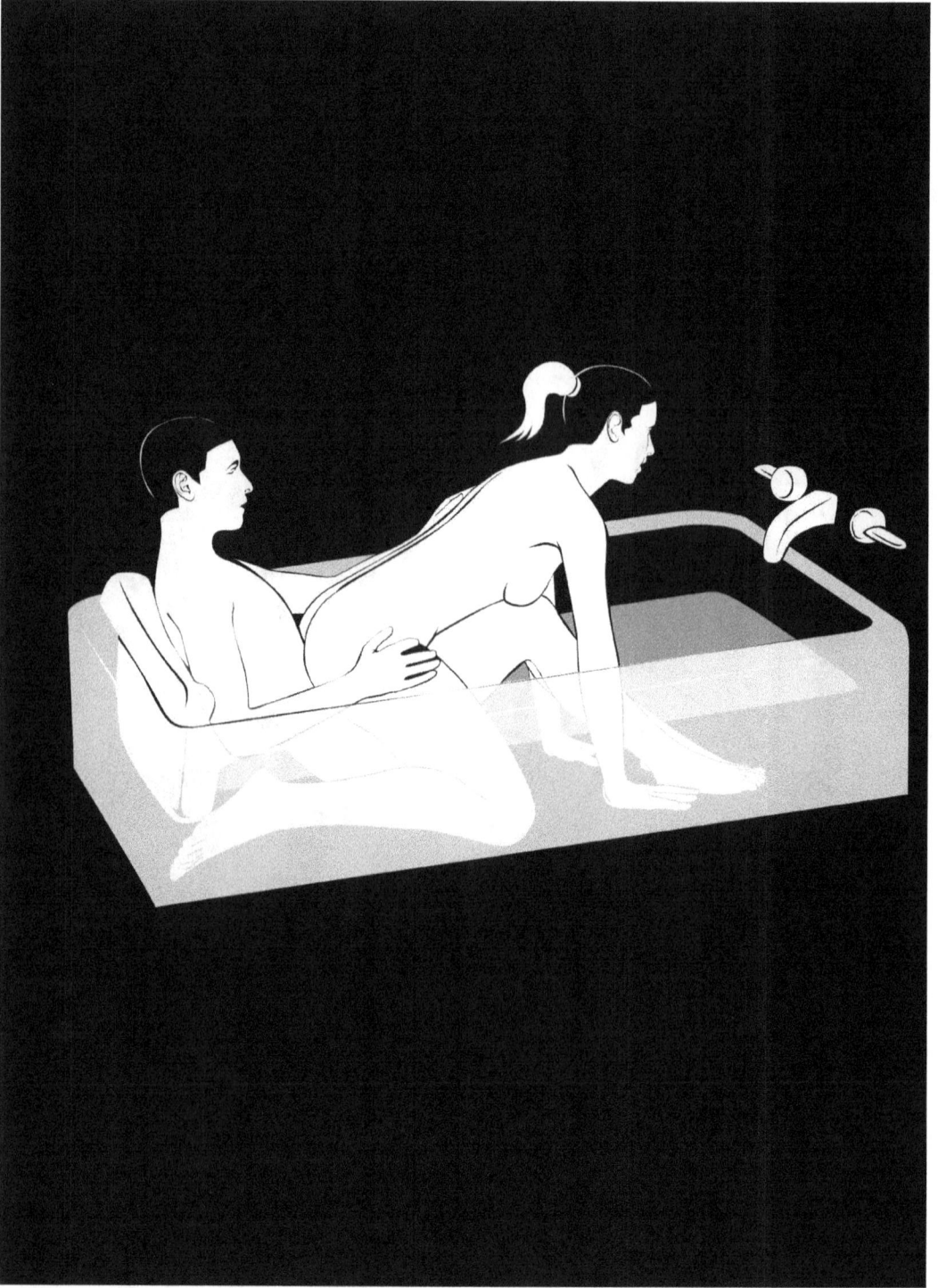

THE SURFBOARD

Fill bathtub halfway, female on top, back to partner, leaning forward and being supported by male's legs.

69
 Mutual oral sex, man on bottom, woman on top.

THE ROCKING HORSE

Male on bottom with his legs crossed and arms outstretched behind him, female straddled on top.

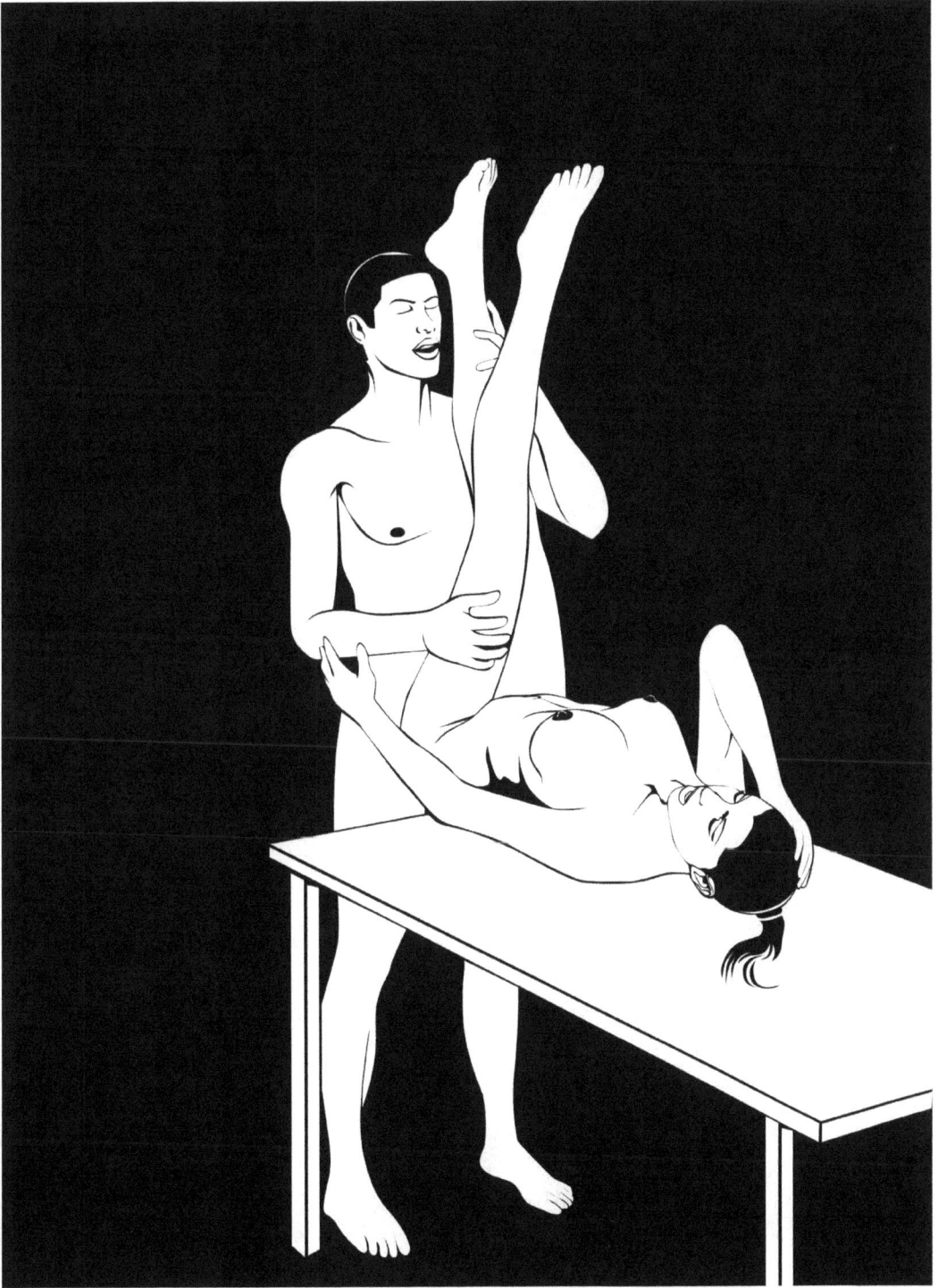

Scissors

Male on top or standing, enters woman while on her side or back, with her legs raised and crossed.

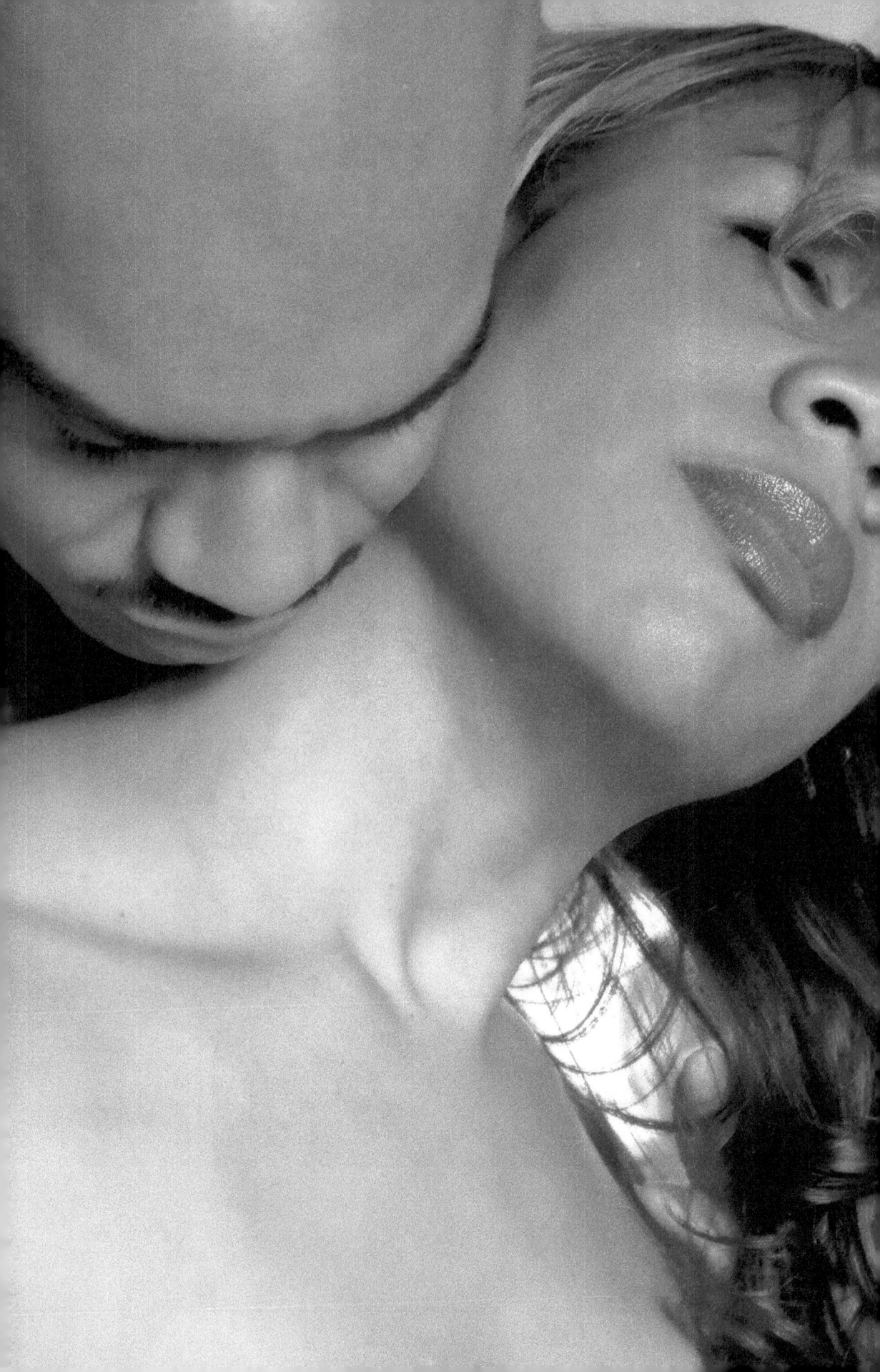

REFINING THE PALATE

Feed Me

There are some people who don't engage in oral sex. I don't understand why a person would deprive himself or herself of such intense pleasure. All of the ingredients for erotic pleasure are packed in this experience: moisture, rhythmic movement, warmth, **sexual abandon**, and direct focus (for the giver and receiver). Lots of sensuality to ignite your passion: taste, smell, touch and sound blend together to create a succulent treat. Watch. Listen to the moans and groan that culminate into screams.

Many people avoid oral sex because they are concerned about hygiene or choking. They find the aroma of the genitals offensive or the hair obtrusive. They fear that it is nasty or inappropriate in some way. There is an easy fix. Groom. Take a shower or bath before oral sex and keep genital hair trimmed to reduce offensive odor and face prickling. For added spice get a Brazilian wax (a procedure that removes nearly all of the pubic hair except for a strip in the center). Yes, fellas, you too! Truth be told, there is more bacteria in a person's mouth than on the genitals. So, if you are willing to kiss your partner, oral sex should not be a problem.

Individuals who fear that oral sex is wrong or inappropriate are likely to have other concerns about freedom of sexual expression. The most important factor to consider is whether or not there are consenting adults making the decision. We are the authorities of our bodies and minds. Unresolved feelings of shame are often associated with rigid ideas or trauma; this can lead to many problems in the bedroom. If you do decide to abstain from oral sex, make sure you do it for your own personal reasons. Ignore the messages that have been handed down by family, friends, or society. *You* are responsible for *your* erotic pleasure.

Technique

If a man is feeding you, and you have a sensitive gag reflex, you can train yourself to prevent choking. Practice on a peeled banana (or some other phallic object). Lick it. It tastes good, resembles the shape and size of an average penis (6 inches), and can provide you with a nutritious snack once you're done.

Be sure to keep the penis moist. Stroke the shaft with your hands, gently tug his scrotum, and massage the prostate (the male g-spot which is located between the scrotum and anus) to provide additional stimulation. Some men even like more direct stimulation of the anus with a lubricated finger. Don't venture back there unless he gives you permission!

Placing a hand on the shaft of the penis will also prevent too much depth. Pulling out just before ejaculation will prevent semen from hitting the back of the throat. Or you can simply ask your partner to alert you to his climax. It is also possible to train yourself to prevent the penis and semen from hitting the back of the throat by pushing the back of the tongue up to the roof of the mouth. If you are not worried about choking and don't mind the taste, swallow for added spice.

This next woman was willing to step outside of her "safety zone." She *"opened up her neck"* to accommodate his needs. Check out the **technique**.

> *"Having oral sex with [fill in the blank], where she explored overriding her gag reflex, and where she assumed the superior position and brought me to orgasm using her vaginal lips."*

This woman's **technique** also hit the spot.

> *"...she was very aggressive with my dick. I like that. We both just wanted to cum as much as we could, anyway we could."*

Masque Sexual Flavors is a product that was specifically developed to conceal the taste of semen. You get to choose what flavor you like: strawberry, chocolate, watermelon, or mango. While it is designed to mask the taste of semen, I imagine it could enhance the flavor of a woman's body too. You might also look in your kitchen for other ingredients that might enrich the flavor. Whipped Cream. Jam. Chocolate syrup.

If a woman is doing the feeding, be mindful of the sensitivity of the clitoris. While this organ provides a lot of pleasure, it can also be the source of pain. Get to know your partner's preferences and then dig in. Use your tongue, lips, and fingers to explore the entire pie. Give attention to the labia minora and labia major (inner and outer lips of the vagina). Enjoy her unique aroma and taste her pleasure. Insert one or two fingers to stimulate the top wall of the vagina. Halfway between the entrance and the cervix, that walnut like object, is the G-spot. If you stroke it just right you might just get to see her cup runneth over. Some women have the capacity to ejaculate or "squirt". So don't be alarmed if you get soaked.

Oral sex is one time that a person gets to focus on his or her own erotic pleasure without having to focus on anyone else. That is unless you are in the 69 position, where you are feeding each other, simultaneously a giver and receiver of pleasure. The best position for receiving oral sex is flat on your back. You don't have to worry where your body parts are, if your legs will give out or when to get off your knees. Just lay back, relax, and feel good. You can use fantasy to excite your mind or just focus on the licking, kissing, tickling, humming, blowing, biting, sucking, nibbling, and lip-smacking goodness. Varying the speed, pressure, and types of movement can also intensify the sensation. Oral sex is love-making by mouth. It does not have to include only the genitals. The moisture and warmth of the tongue and mouth can be used to stimulate the entire body. Lay back and let your partner love you.

One woman wrote about her experience during oral sex. *"Stimulation of the clitoris and vagina"* created intense levels of **arousal** and produces a physiological response that represents excitement (i.e., vaginal lubrication); *"the juices were flowing."*

The above recipe left a lot to the imagination, because there are several ways to stimulate the clitoris and vagina. This next woman however, gives step-by-step instruction.

"He was going down on me and teasing me and not using his finger so I asked him if he wanted to "do it." He slides me off to the side of the bed and spreads my legs and starts tapping the head of his penis by the opening of my vagina. Man did that stir some great feelings up. He continued to do that for a few more minutes while I was playing with my clitoris. He finally penetrated me and within minutes I had an ORGASM!"

Lastly, a woman wrote, *"He ate pussy good as hell."* Simply put, good **technique** leads to high **arousal**.

Choose Your Flavors: Oral Sex

INDEPENDENT STUDY.

Look at your Specialty Ingredients on page **82**. Think about your experience as a giver and receiver of oral pleasure. What ingredients do you keep? What ingredients do you remove from your *recipe for ecstasy*? Use "I" statements to communicate your preferences. For example, "I like the way you stroke my penis as you lick the tip" or "I dislike giving oral pleasure when you are not groomed".

Chef's Notes on Oral Sex...

I like... _____

_____

_____

I dislike... _____

_____

_____

Sous Chef's Notes on Oral Sex...

I like... _____

_____

_____

I dislike... _____

_____

_____

COOKING CLASS ASSIGNMENT.

Now, work together on a recipe card that combines your abilities, wants and needs for oral sex.

Couple's Recipe for Oral Sex

Couple's Recipe for Oral Sex

CATERING & SPECIAL OCCASIONS

Even the most humble restaurants have the capacity to do things differently for special occasions. This takes planning, organization, and attention to details. Make space for culinary delights in your home kitchen and away from home.

Special moments, as a couple, bring opportunities for **newness** and **focus on other.** Cater to each other. Make fantasies come true with **meaningful moments**.

Support Staff

Every relationship needs a group of supporters. More specifically, a good babysitter or list of supporters is needed if you have children. Date night, stay night, day trips, and vacations without the children are necessary to give couples the opportunity to focus on each other and themselves with undivided attention. Most often when I ask couples, *"When was the last time you spent time alone with your mate?"* The response is *"It's been a while"* or *"I can't even remember the last time."* If this is you, then it has been too long. Make a list of people you trust to care for your children. Then use it!

COUPLE'S SUPPORT STAFF		
NAME	**PHONE**	**EMAIL**

HOME COOKING

As a clinical psychologist and sexologist, I have encountered parents who have neglected their couplehood. The relationship is sacrificed for the needs of the family. The family unit requires constant feeding. Sadly, exclusive focus on family can lead to neglect of the couple and, thus, the demise of the couple's relationship. After investing many years in the family, a person may one day awake disconnected and feel they are lying next to a stranger.

Don't forget the person you were before you became married with children. Individuals should spend time preserving a strong sense of self. This whole person will contribute to the entity that is "us." There's you, there's me and there's us. The "us" is the foundation of the family. If a family is to survive, the couple has to invest in and protect their union. One way to accomplish this is to spend time together. Really together. For those of you who have children, these exercises were written with you in mind. You can be parents *and* have a healthy loving connection.

Create an experience of **awayness**. If you are not ready for a getaway, aim for something less daunting. A quickie or "staycation" while the kids are at a playdate or school. That's right. Take a vacation day together while the kids go to school. Make *your* home *your* getaway. Carve out time and do something simple to nurture your relationship. Think about your favorite aspects of vacation and recreate them in your home – be it food, music, losing track of time. Disconnect from the world and reconnect with each other.

Staycation

If you are creating a staycation, you have to work extra hard to remove the presence of your daily life. This means putting away the laptops (unless you are watching movies), silencing the phones, create an out-of-office reply for work calls and emails. Don't think about the chores or bills. For parents, yes, this includes getting rid of your kids. Go to that list of support staff that you have already created (see p. 107). On your staycation, consider some touristy things (nature walks, art galleries, museums, restaurants) or just stay in bed all day and order takeout. The only thing that matters is that you spend some **intentional time** together.

Staying in doesn't have to be boring. Listen to this woman describe a stimulating night at home full of **variety** and **multiple orgasm**.

> *"One night I was relaxing with my husband. I got dressed up for him [and] we got drunk … We had sex all night long. We watched porno movies, had oral, vaginal and anal sex. We also used toys to enhance the experience. I lost count of how many times I had an orgasm."*

After a disappointing marriage, this next woman had to do a complete overhaul of her kitchen. She applied many of the ingredients to the *recipe for ecstasy* including **nature of the relationship, newness, passion, intimacy**, and **mood** (satiety). **Awayness** proved to be one of the essential ingredients to this recipe. She got away from an abusive relationship and went away with her new lover.

"While I was married, sex was terrible, uncomfortable, painful ... I became quite disgusted by my then-husband. I was also experiencing emotional and verbal abuse. I cannot remember a time ever with him that I reached orgasm through vaginal penetration. I think I only reached orgasm 30% of the time and that was direct from either his hand or mouth (or by my hand when he was away). I have been in a long distance relationship now for about a year. I have never felt this strong an emotional connection to anyone in my life. Nor have I ever, until him, felt true sexual attraction to a man. I didn't know I could. The second mini-vacation I took to spend with him out of state I was able to reach orgasm through vaginal penetration. Feeling him under me, hearing his voice and his moans, as he started to cum I realized I was actually close and his increased reaction drove mine higher. As he was breathing, "I'm cumming," I was so overwhelmed and surprised all I could say was "Me too, me too." I rode him a little harder and faster until we were both finished and were spent. I collapsed on his chest and just giggled at myself as he held me."

Need more inspiration? An elegant night out inspired this hot night in.

"After a fancy night out, got home, almost ripped each other's clothes off and had HOT sex."

Stay Night

If you can't manage a whole week or weekend, then a *stay night* will do. If you have children, send them on an overnight with friends or family. If you don't have kids, you can get right down to the business of deciding how you are going to spend your night in together. Use your recipe cards – learn from the previous work that you have done. **Mutual Pleasure** might be on the menu. Skip ahead and *Put Something New on the Menu*. Or it can be something as simple as ordering take-out and playing board games.

Stay night easily transitions into *play night* (sex play that is). While staying in and cuddling is always on the menu, play night is a great alternative and/or addition.

Play Night

After your first hours of the evening, designate the remainder of the time for sex play. No rules, responsibilities, or expectations, just plain old fun. If you are like this next couple, a night filled with **anticipation**, romance (**mood**), and **variety** might just hit the spot.

"[A] whole night alone with my partner. We had dinner, we flirted, and we had a couple of alcoholic beverages. We got home and the mood was very romantic. I asked him to take me to bed and we proceeded to kiss. We kissed and touched for a long while and we traded oral favors. It was very sensual. Then we had intercourse till I reached climax. Then again, and again, until he reached orgasm. We then held one another all night."

This next child-free couple's Saturday night had all the necessary fixings including **timing, passion, variety** (oral sex, positions), **communication**, and **intense orgasms**.

"Saturday night sex with my husband prior to getting pregnant and having a child. On Saturdays we used to have a lot of energy, were able to be spontaneous, blast music, have a few drinks, and get lost in our sexual passion. We could have a lengthy period of foreplay, sexual talk, oral sex, and build up the tension toward intercourse. We would switch positions and move around the house [floor, sofa, bed, shower]. And intercourse would culminate with very powerful orgasms–sometimes I could have more than one, but not always."

Dine In
COOKING CLASS ASSIGNMENT.
Document what you enjoy about staying in and pick a date!

Chef's Notes on Staying In...

_____
_____
_____
_____
_____
_____
_____
_____

Sous Chef's Notes on Staying In...

_____
_____
_____
_____
_____
_____
_____
_____

Couple's Recipe for Staying In

Date Night will be: _____

Have a Tasting Party

Approach this next exercise as if you want to design a dream kitchen. Don't let finances limit you. If you can't afford the time or money for full renovations, then you can improve on one aspect at a time. Take care to select the desired components and put them together to create a space that is safe and comfortable. No, you are not actually going to redesign your kitchen. However, I want you to start thinking about your hopes and dreams. Maybe you want to go on a week-long cooking retreat in Tuscany or cruise to the South of France. Focus on building the *dream* for now and then start stacking away your chips so that you can afford it later.

When building your dream vacation, keep in mind that this is something that you and your partner are going to work towards together. If money is an issue, start saving now. In a true union, everyone has value, no matter how much money they bring to the table. Pick a dollar amount you can contribute monthly, put it all in one pot, and get ready to pack your bags. Where do you want to go? What do you want to see?

In the meantime, start with a weekend getaway. It can be to a neighboring city or state. Rely on local publications to find free events nearby.

INDEPENDENT STUDY.

Design a weekend getaway. Try something simple before you move to sensational. Pick a place, method of travel, sights to see separately and/or together. Don't forget the necessary supplies (toys, lubricant, sexy attire) for pleasure-making. Create a narrative and share it with your partner. Then the two of you can design a weekend getaway that reflects both of your tastes.

Chef's Notes on a Weekend Getaway...

Sous Chef's Notes on a Weekend Getaway...

COOKING CLASS ASSIGNMENT.

Combine your notes from the previous independent study and pick a date.

Couple's Recipe for a Weekend Getaway

Our weekend getaway will be:: _____

From Simple to Sensational

INDEPENDENT STUDY.

Now that you have successfully planned a weekend getaway, you should have a structure to follow when creating your dream vacation. Did you take turns choosing a trip from your respective lists? Or did you start with the Couple's Recipe? Did you plan too many activities without making time for much needed rest? Use your weekend getaway as a springboard to take you from simple to sensational. Now, don't get overwhelmed by the long list of things to do when planning a vacation; remember you have the rest of your life to figure this out. Take time to save the money, pick the location, and make your dreams a reality.

Chef's Notes on a Dream Vacation...

_____
_____
_____
_____
_____
_____
_____

Sous Chef's Notes on a Dream Vacation...

_____
_____
_____
_____
_____
_____
_____
_____

COOKING CLASS ASSIGNMENT.

Combine your notes from the previous independent study and pick a date.

Couple's Recipe for a Dream Vacation

Our dream vacation will be:: _____

PUT SOMETHING NEW ON THE MENU

The next series of activities will primarily focus on two ingredients **newness** and **variety**. These two ingredients are essential to maintaining **passion** in long-term relationships. In my research and therapeutic work with couples, I have found that passion is difficult to sustain. How do we get passion back in a long-term relationship? Tap into a time when things were not so serious. Let go of your responsibilities and inhibitions. **Sexual abandon** is not the only objective. **Intimacy, mood, communication, mutuality**, and trust are also on the menu. If a *safe* **mood** is created, it will encourage your walls to come down enough for you to connect with your partner in a meaningful way.

Try something new! Start with something easy. You are dining out at a new restaurant and you can't pick your staple off the menu. Pick something new; be adventurous. This woman noted that this was the first time she was had for supper, and she wrote:

> "One weekend I came home from school and my fiancé and I were hooking up for a sexual encounter before I headed back. This was during our dating. I was so excited every time we got together. It was a new relationship for me. He began to perform oral sex on me. This was the first time he had done this to me, so that made it all the more fun. What really turned me on was when I looked down at him, he had a towel tucked in his shirt like a bib, and it was suppertime."

she added,

> "... He was being freaky and I liked it."

Sexploration: Mutual Sexting

The experience of anonymity makes people say and do things that they normally would not. It creates an opportunity to step outside of one's comfort zone and get a little wild.

INDEPENDENT STUDY.

In this exercise, take your time.

- Think of the kinkiest, most adventurous, sexy, lustful messages.
- Write them down. How does it feel seeing them in writing?
- Send one a day to your partner for a week.
- At the end of the week, check your temperature throughout the day. Are you getting warmer?

While not the best way to address interpersonal conflict, text messaging *can* be used to add fun and excitement to a relationship. *Sex messages* serve as foreplay, helping to build **anticipation** for love making. You may find that messaging is easier than talking. It can provide the opening needed to start a dialogue about your sexual fantasies. At the same time, you may feel uncomfortable or embarrassed having explicit sexual thoughts and, even moreso, writing them down and sharing them with your partner. If this is your experience, take some time to understand the source of this discomfort. It may emanate from old messages received when you were growing up. Or it may simply be the angst associated with trying something new. Give yourself the opportunity to grow; growth is never easy or comfortable.

Now, find a private place to write down those steamy messages ... and don't forget to share!

COOKING CLASS ASSIGNMENT.

Critique your experience. What did you like about it? What are some things that you might do differently? What was it like sharing in this way?

Chef's Notes on Sexting Partner...

What I liked ... _____

_____

What I Might Do Differently... _____

_____

My Thoughts on Sexting... _____

_____

_____

Sous Chef's Notes on Sexting Partner...

What I liked ... _____

_____

What I Might Do Differently... _____

_____

My Thoughts on Sexting... _____

_____

_____

Sexploration: Picnic for Lovers

Prepare a meal together. First decide on the day and time. Create the menu. Carefully select the ingredients. Individuals bring unique characteristics to relationships. Based on your respective qualities and preference, decide if you will shop together or separately.

One person may take the lead as the Chef, while the other occupies the position of Sous Chef. Divide the tasks based on your strengths and prepare your dish. Be sure to have dessert. The menu should consist of easy, sensuous choices. Finger foods sound like fun. Pay attention to how well you work together as a team. Compromise. Focus on working cooperatively from start to finish. Yes, that means kitchen clean-up too.

Use the **setting** to create a **mood**. Make it sexy or romantic. Make enough dinner for two, with a setting for one. The place-setting should be put on the blanket you have laid out in the middle of the living room or dining room floor. Use only one plate, one glass, one fork, one knife, and one napkin. For those who can't bear to share utensils, your hands will do. Feed each other. If it's really good, go back for seconds! For added spice, get naked and enjoy the picnic for lovers; blindfold the receiver, role-play and create a theme (e.g. "You are my prisoner").

Take this next savory soliloquy, where the woman takes time to have more than just a good meal. She created a relaxing **setting** and a romantic **mood**. The night was full of **intimacy** and **mutuality**.

> *"We had plans to get together one day to relax and watch T.V. Well, I had other things on my mind. Before he arrived I moved all the furniture to one side of the living room, therefore leaving an open space. I put a blanket on the floor, had candle lit, and a cold bottle of wine. I also had on a sexy nightie. When he arrived he had Chinese food in his arms; we had an indoor picnic on the floor. After eating, I couldn't control myself. I removed his clothing and caressed his body; he kindly returned the favor. Then we made love on the blanket. The session was very intense and wonderful. Afterwards he cuddled [me] until we fell asleep. It was a great evening; however, we still never managed to watch T.V."*

COOKING CLASS ASSIGNMENT.

Critique your experience. What did you like about it? What are some things that you might do differently? What was it like sharing in this way?

Chef's Notes on Picnic for Lovers...

What I liked ... _____

_____

_____

What I Might Do Differently... _____

_____

_____

My Thoughts on Picnicing... _____

_____

_____

Sous Chef's Notes on Picnic for Lovers...

What I liked ... _____

_____

_____

What I Might Do Differently... _____

_____

_____

My Thoughts on Picnicing... _____

_____

_____

Sexploration: Kiss the Cook

A long wet kiss is the appetizer to a satisfying meal. Pecking is the kiss of convenience. While it serves its purpose when you are trying to get out the door quickly, a peck on the cheek should never be substituted for "a real kiss." Pecks are for chickens: people who are too afraid to open up.

When you get a peck, request a "real kiss" – one that requires intention. You have to slow down and allow your lips and tongue to co-mingle. Embrace.

> In the wooing phase and in the prelude to the act of love, the mouth is rediscovered as an organ of pleasure and the entire skin surface is suffused with sensual joy. Longing sees its oldest posture, the embrace (Fraiberg, 1971).

Take time to explore your lover's mouth with your tongue and teeth. Open your mouth and initiate a romantic moment. Hold and be held. Pursed lips, that never part to make room for deep passionate kisses, leave you wanting. Don't get stuck in the pecking rut.

You never know where you might end up when the night starts with a passionate kiss. In the next series of narratives, rubbing lips together ignited **passion**.

> *"When this girl [unexpectedly] told me to 'shut-up and kiss me.' We start ripping our clothes off and start having sex on my living room floor and all the way to the bedroom leaving a trail of clothes to the bedroom, like breadcrumbs."*

From passionate kissing to genital kisses this next recipe sure hits the spot!

> *"My mate and I started passionately kissing as soon as we saw each other. Clothes peeled off and he led me to the bedroom. We kissed, hugged, and he sucked every part of my body, bringing me to a hard orgasm with his mouth. Then he "slow grinded" me, but would "bang" me hard at times. We did all types of positions with him pulling out to orally satisfy me in between ... this went on for about an hour. PERFECT!!!"*

COOKING CLASS ASSIGNMENT.

Not everyone is a natural kisser. Some people don't even like it. There may be changes that you want to make to this very intimate form of relating. Be thoughtful as you tweak this aspect of your recipe. What do you like about kissing? Tell your partner about your favorite kiss or, better yet, show him.

Chef's Notes on a Kissing...

_____

_____

_____

_____

_____

_____

Sous Chef's Notes on Kissing...

_____

_____

_____

_____

_____

_____

Sexploration: Field Trip!

Take a trip to the novelty store (online or in person). Be sure to make a list and check it twice. It doesn't matter if you are naughty or nice. Make sure you both have things that will add flavor and **variety** to your *recipe for ecstasy*. Lingerie, underwear, perfume, toys, movies, cattails, fuck-me pumps, costumes for role-play.

Go to a club for adult entertainment. That's right, a place where there are mostly nude dancers putting on a show for your own personal pleasure. It sure added spice to this night.

> *"The most satisfying sexual experience has been with my husband. We have been together (as a couple, not married) for 21 years. There was a period of time when sex was just sporadic; time of day, place didn't matter. There are many situations that I could speak on; the most satisfying times are after a mystery date night when we pleasure ourselves via strip clubs etc. and the aftermath is always magical."*

COOKING CLASS ASSIGNMENT.

Do your research and create a shopping list to guide you. Locate venues that might satisfy your sensual appetite. Be adventurous, try skinny dipping or wine tasting.

CHEF'S GROCERY LIST

My Ingredients for a Field Trip, Ideas & Locations

SOUS CHEF'S GROCERY LIST

My Ingredients for a Field Trip, Ideas & Locations

Sexploration: Dance for me Baby

Erotic movement can be a source of great excitement. It engages many of the senses: sight, sound, and touch. If you get close enough to your partner you can even invite smell and taste.

COOKING CLASS ASSIGNMENT.

Think about the music you are going to use for your personal performance. If you need inspiration, you can get some from the playlists provided in Appendix B through D. Dress in sexy attire. Dance as if no one is watching. In reality, you may literally have a captive audience. Handcuff or tie up your mate to test the limits of trust in your relationship. This exercise is meant to be fun and sexy. You should be free from judgment and expectation. Allow yourself to express your love and sensuality with movement.

What was it like being the center of attention? How did you feel watching your partner?

Chef's Notes on Dancing...
Being the Dancer... _____

_____

Watchng My Partner Dance... _____

_____

_____

Sous Chef's Notes on Dancing...
Being the Dancer... _____

_____

_____

Watchng My Partner Dance... _____

_____

_____

Rate the New Menu

COOKING CLASS ASSIGNMENT.

Think about the past five sexploration activities. Did you have a 5-star dining experience? Something too hot, too cold, too spicy, just right? Don't let the memories from the previous pages slip away. Capture your experience with words, pictures, and/or video. These things can be used in the future. Create a narrative about what worked and what didn't work so that you can refer to it as you tweak your *recipe for ecstasy.*

Chef's Notes on Sexploration Activities...

Chef's Notes on Sexploration Activities...

LEFT OVERS

Love is salubrious – it makes us healthier. As a single ingredient however, it is not enough to maintain **intimacy** and **passion** in long-term relationships. Long-term sexual and relationship satisfaction requires hard work and **commitment**. True satisfaction – ecstasy – is a space and time that we occupy when our alliance is functioning at its peak.

Ecstasy does not "just happen." We create it! Often, people enter into unions with grandiose expectations of one another. "Be my lover, friend, confidant, companion, partner, spouse, advisor." The list of demands is never-ending, like an insatiable appetite. It is unrealistic to seek flawlessness in a person who has limits. While you should expect your partner to come to the table with offerings, s/he is not solely responsible for feeding you. Each person must also know how to fend for thyself.

Thus, the recipe begins with the "self."

In order to make good love that will last a life-time, a person must first have obtained a sense of self. That is, a sense of individuality that thrives on separateness. Being separate from others enables a whole person to exist with full awareness of personal ideas, hopes, boundaries, feelings, likes, and dislikes. It is this awareness that conveys our individual tastes. With this knowledge we are equipped to seek out the ingredients that will meet our needs. Now we can create a *recipe for ecstasy*.

In separation there needs to be a comfortable distance. A vantage point where you are able to see each others' desires, while staying connected to one's self, one's own yearning. There is a selfishness that exists in the face of **mutuality**. A place where self and other co-exist. A union.

We seek long-term relationships for security, dependence, stability, longevity, safety. These are all stabilizing forces that, ironically, may actually extinguish the flame of passion. **Passion**, one of the most difficult ingredients to maintain over time, calls for the excitement of **newness**, the distance of **awayness**, and the freedom of **sexual abandon**. Infuse your relationship with **variety** by recreating your recipe over and over. Continue to share your personal nuances as they change over the life-span.

Set a **mood**; build anticipation. **Arouse** each other's curiosity. Let the tension build as you **engender feelings** of longing. The best foreplay is the time you spend together focused on building esteem (**positive self- regard**) and **communicating** your appreciation for the invaluable investment of one's self. In this instance it is not about **technique** or **timing**. Instead, it is about sharing and building. Mixing together the **ingredients of self** with the **ingredients of other** in order to yield an erotic fusion.

Allow yourself to extend far beyond the throes of **orgasm**, yet remain within bounds and respect the **nature of your relationship**. You now have parameters that define your desires and dislikes. If you lose your connection, use the work you have done here to find your way back. Own your individuality and always stay true to one another. This is a delicate balance.

Only you and your partner get to decide what's on the menu. *Create a recipe for ecstasy!*

Appendix A: Sexual Satisfaction Questionnaire

Please answer the following questions as openly and honestly as possible. Take all the time you need. Please use the paper provided and number your responses to match this sheet. If you need more writing space, ask the examiner for more paper.

- 1. In as much detail as possible, please describe the most sexually satisfying experience of your life.

- 2. What made this experience so satisfying?

- 3a. What was the nature of your relationship with the partner in the experience you have just described?
  a. One Night-Stand/ Anonymous/ Experimental *[If "a", continue to Question #4.]
  b. Casual Dating
  c. Spouse/Committed Relationship
  d. Other, describe _____

- 3b. If you responded to question [3a] with b, c, or d, answer the following questions:
  a. How long have you been involved with this partner?
  b. How often do you have sex with this partner?
  c. How often would you like to have sex with this partner?

- 4. During the experience you have just described, how did you feel about yourself and how did you feel about your partner? That is, what feelings were aroused?

- 5. During the experience you have just described, did you reach orgasm? If so, what do you recall about that experience?

- 6. Have you ever considered having a child[ren] with this partner? Why or why not?

Appendix B: Romance Playlist

Hope That We Can
Be Together Soon . . . . Christopher Williams featuring Miki Howard

Dealing. . . . . Eric Robertson featuring Lalah Hathaway

Ingredients of Love . . . . Angie Stone featuring Musiq

Justin Chillin' . . . . Norman Brown featuring Miki Howard

Love Changes. . . . . Kashif & Kashif featuring Meli'sa Morgan

What You Do. . . . . Chrisette Michele featuring Ne-Yo

Nothing Has Ever Felt Like This. . . . . Rachelle Ferrel featuring Will Downing

You Belong to Me. . . . . Chaka Khan featuring Michael McDonald

I'll be Good . . . . Angela Winbush & Renee

Crusie Control. . . . . Teena Marie & Smokey Robinson

Part II . . . . Jay Z featuring Beyoncé

If It's Love . . . . Kem featuring Chrisette Michele

Tell Me All About it. . . . . Michael Franks featuring Laura Fygi

Fallin (remix) . . . . Alicia Keys, Busta Rhymes, & Rampage

Back Together Again. . . . . Roberta Flack & Donny Hathaway

As . . . . Marsha Ambrosius & Anthony Hamilton

You Got Me . . . . The Roots featuring Erykah Badu

Feeling The Way. Norman Brown featuring Chante Moore

Stay . . . . Ledisi featuring Jaheim

Lay Your Troubles Down. . . . . Angela Winbush featuring Ronald Isley

So In Love . . . . Jill Scott featuring Anthony Hamilton

Love Duet . . . . Michael Franks featuring unknown artist

Fire & Desire . . . . Rick James & Teena Marie

Love of My Life. . . . . Eryka Badu & Common

Valentine Love . . . . John Henderson & Jean Carn

Tonight, I Celebrate My Love. . . . . Peabo Bryson & Roberta Flack

Beautiful . . . . Mariah Carey featuring Miguel

Candlelight and You . . . . Chanté Moore & Keith Washington

Endless Love. . . . . Diana Ross & Lionel Richie

Latch . . . . Disclosure featuring Sam Smith

I Love You . . . . Christopher Washington & Chanté Moore

Appendix C: Pole/Lap Dance Playlist

My Man	Santana featuring Mary J. Blige & Big Boi
Shakin' it 4 Daddy	Robin Thicke featuring Nicki Minaj
Love More	Chris Brown fearuring Ayden
Imaginary Playmates	Angela Winbush & Rene
Love Calls (remix)	Kem & Floetry
Do You Love What You Feel	Rufus & Chaka Khan
Closer I Get	Beyoncé & Luther Vandross
Loveeeeeee Song	Rihanna & Future
Amore (Sexo)	Santana featuring Macy Gray
Drop it Low	Ester Dean & Chris Brown
Give It Up To Me	Sean Paul & Keisha Cole
What's It Gonna Be	Busta Rhymes & Janet Jackson
Dirty	Christina Aguilera featuring Redman
I (Who Have Nothing)	Luther Vandross featuring Martha Walsh
Whenever You Call	Brian Mcknight & Mariah Carey
Body Part (remix)	Ciara featuring Future & B.O.B.
Bad	Wale featuring Tiara Thomas
Drunk in Love	Beyoncé featuring Jay Z
Fool for You	Cee Lo Green featuring Melanie Fiona
What's Your Fantasy	Ludacris & Shawna
Superhuman	Chris Brown featuring Keri Hilson
Motivation	Kelly Rowland featuring Lil Wayne
Promise	Ciara featuring R. Kelly
Turn your Lights Down Low	Bob Marly & Lauryn Hill
Oh	Ciara featuring Ludacris
So Good	Davina featuring Raekwon
Thank God I found You	Joe featuring Mariah Carey & Nas
Rush Over	Marcus Miller & Me'shell Ndegeocello
Fire We Make	Alicia Keys featuring Maxwell
Dark Horse	Katy Perry featuring Juicy J
It Won't Stop	Sevyn Streeter featuring Chris Brown
Down on Me	Jeremih & 50 Cent

Appendix D: Variety is The Spice of Life Playlist

SLOW JAMS:

What I'm Trying to Say	Phillippe
Number One Hit	R. Kelly
Love Bath	Smokey Robinson
Share My Life	Kem
Best of Me	Anthony Hamilton
Woman	Raheem DeVaughn
The Way You Love Me	Michael Jackson
I Need Love	Robin Thicke
Desire	Jose James
Remember	Me'shell Ndegeocello
All About Our Love	Sadé

FUNKY:

Dontcha	The Internet
Stay	The Controllers
Blow	Beyoncé
Tonight (Best you Ever Had)	John Legend featuring Ludacris
I Want You	Phil Perry
Feels So Right	Janet Jackson
Secrets	Maroon 5
Hard Candy	Madonna
Lick	Joi
Kisses Down Low	Kelly Rowland
Slave to the Rhythm	Michael Jackson

Appendix E: Erectile Dysfunction is not a Death Sentence

The humiliation and sense of loss that comes with sexual dysfunction often prevents disclosure of symptoms and inquiry regarding treatment. This article will outline the various causes of erectile dysfunction (ED) and treatments available for ED including current medications (Viagra, Levetra, and Cialis), penile injection, urethral suppository, vacuum pump, and penile implants. Let us not forget one of the most important and often disregarded forms of treatment: psychotherapy.

ED is defined as a persist inability in attain and maintain an erection sufficient for sexual activity. It has many causes: psychological (anxiety, depression, trauma); behavioral (drug use, smoking, obesity); and physiological (medication, prostate surgery, injury, aging). There are also several different treatments for ED. Choosing the right form of treatment may be intimidating. It is always best to consult with a professional when trying to address this problem. A urologist can discuss the medical treatments (physical therapies, medications, surgeries) and a psychologist can assist with the personal and relational strategies.

Behavioral Remedies

Physicians always start with ruling out other causes of a dysfunction. That is the path of least resistance. If the condition is caused by something like medication, obesity, or excessive alcohol use, the solution is technically simple: change the medication and/or change your behavior. This is sometimes easier said than done. Be sure to partner with your physician and other treatment providers to find a safe, sustainable strategy.

Physical Therapy Remedies

Penis Rings. For men who can achieve an erection, but have difficulty maintaining it, the use of a penis ring (also referred to as cock ring) may alleviate the problem. This mechanism is placed at the base of a flaccid penis. After arousal, it slows the flow of blood out of an erect penis, resulting in maintaining an erection.

Kegel Exercises. Kegel exercises could also be included in a treatment regimen for ED. This exercise supports sexual health by strengthening the pelvic floor muscles and encouraging blood flow to the genitals. There are also masturbatory exercises that may improve body awareness.

Penis Pump. The penis pump is a cylinder that fits over the penis and creates a vacuum around the penis. This device can be operated manually or electrically. The vacuum created by the pump draws blood into the shaft and holds the pressure by a penis ring to maintain an erection. If a pump is used incorrectly it can damage penile tissue. Some other drawbacks to this method of treatment include inconvenience, limited rigidity, and discomfort.

Medical Remedies

Oral Medications. Advances in technology and medicine have increased the options for men living with erectile dysfunction. As a result of advertising, most people are aware of the pharmaceutical options available to treat ED. Viagra class medications work by increasing the responsiveness of the erectile tissue to nitric oxide, the neurotransmitter that is chiefly responsible for penile erection (Levy and Baldwin, 2012). While these drugs are easily accessed and convenient, they come with risk. If combined with certain other drugs, they can be life-threatening.

Other Medications. Erectile injections and suppositories are the treatment of choice when penile nerves have been damaged by prostate surgery or injury. Some medications produce an erection by injecting a hormone (alprostadil) directly into the penis tissue. The alprostadil suppository is a soft pellet that is inserted directly into the urethra. These methods work by opening up the blood vessels and allowing blood to flow into the penis. Some men may not find these treatments appealing because of the potential for pain or discomfort. There are also other limitations such as the number of days per week they can be used and co-occurring health problems that prohibit the use of these methods.

Surgery. Surgical options are often presented when other medical treatment is unsuccessful. That is, of course, if you can afford it. Often the procedure is cost-prohibitive. Some insurance companies such as Medicare may cover the expense (or some of it) if the procedure meets the criteria for "medical necessity." This is likely to vary from company to company.

First generation penile prosthetics/implants were hard to live with (pun intended), because of the fact that they gave a man a permanent erection. This method uses a semi-rigid plastic rod that keeps the penis permanently stiff enough for intercourse (Levy and Baldwin, 2012). This semi-rigid implant would need to be bent down after intercourse to conceal its presence. This doesn't sound like a pleasant option and may lead to more humiliation about ED.

Another option is the three-piece inflatable implant. The implant is made of a pair of cylinders that are placed in the erection chamber, a pump is placed in the scrotum, and a fluid filled reservoir is placed in the abdomen (in a space next to the bladder). So far, the reviews of this product have been positive. While there have been some complaints about problems with deflation, many men boast about feeling like they are in their twenties again. I can imagine that this method of treatment would be preferred over the pump or penile injection, which often ruins the mood. Keep in mind, these surgical procedures are not reversible.

Psychological Remedies

Psychological treatments should be considered as an adjunct to the aforementioned treatments. If there is not some clear medical cause of ED, a therapist may be helpful in identifying sources of anxiety, depression, and trauma that may affect symptoms. Some professionals recommend a talking therapy early in the process, as it is perceived as less medically less intrusive than medications or surgeries.

Even if there is a clear medical correlate, psychotherapy can assist a person in making life-altering changes and in coping with an experience of loss which often accompanies ED. Whatever the cause and course of treatment, erectile dysfunction is not a death sentence; you can still achieve sexual satisfaction.

Appendix F: Optional Spice

RECOMMENDED READING

Carter, M. & Carter, L. (2004). Completely Overcome Vaginismus: The practical approach to pain-free intercourse. Book 1 & 2.

Heiman, J.R., Lopiccolo, L. & Lopiccolo, J. (1987). Becoming Orgasmic.

Means, M. (2012). The Recipe for Ecstasy What Women Want: Sexual and Relationship Satisfaction.

Means, Myrtle. (2013). Erectile Dysfunction is not a Death Sentence.
Available at www.therecipeforecstasy.com

McCarthy, B.W., and Metz, M.E. (2004). Coping with Erectile Dysfunction: How to regain confidence and enjoy great sex.

EROTIC LITERATURE

Spicy / Contemporary

Shades of Grey Series, E.L. James
Black Dagger Brotherhood Series, J.R. Ward

Staple /Classic

Tropic of Cancer and other titles, Henry Miller
Delta of Venus and other titles, Anais Nin

VIDEOS

Sinclair Videos (Live Better Love Better Video Series, Kama Sutra)

Sizzle Series (The Art of Oral Loving, The Art of Self Pleasuring)

Zanes Sex Chronicles

Sock It To Me

Café Amore

MAGAZINES

Online or paperback

Hustler

PentHouse

Playgirl

WEBSITES

www.therecipeforecstasy.com

www.sinclairinstitute.org

www.adamevetoys.com

www.loverslane.com

www.bedroomkandi.com

www.bettersex.com

www.vaginismus.com

www.lelo.com

TOYS DECADENCE/ HIGH END

Lelo Sex Toys

- •Gigi 2
- •Ida
- •Smart Wand Large

Bedroom Kandi Sex Toys

- •Happiness & Joy
- •Kandipop
- •Love Me Naughty

Torc II C Ring

Restraint System

Penis Pump

Leberator Esse (sex chair)

TOYS DIET/ LOW END

Head Honcho Masturbator

Maximus Enhancement Ring

Scented Candles

Sex Wedge or Cushion

Handcuffs

Rabbit

Cattails

Anal beads

Massage Oil

Feather Tickler

Ben Wa Balls

ROLE-PLAY THEMES

Strangers

Bondage

Good Girl - Bad Boy

Stripper

Photographer

Fitness Instructor

Doctor - Patient

Call Girl

References

Barbach, L. (2001). For Each Other: Sharing sexual intimacy. New York: Signet

Erikson, E. (1963). Childhood and Society, 2nd Edfition. New York: Norton.

Firestone, R. W., Firestone, L. A., & Catlett, J. (2006). Suggestions for enhancing sexual intimacy. In R. W Firestone, L. A. Firestone, J. Catlett (Eds.), Sex and Love in Intimate Relationships (pp. 263-279).

Fraiberg, S. (1971). How a Baby Learns to Love. Redbook Magazine, 76:164-171.

Kaplan, H. S. (1974). The New Sex Therapy:Active treatment of sexual dysfunction. New York: Brunner/Mazel.

Levy, S. and Baldwin, J. (2012) Human Sexuality, 4th Edition. Sunderland, MA: Sinauer Associates.

Masters, W. H., Johnson, V. E., Kolodny, R. C. (1986) Masters and Johnson on Sex and Human Loving. Boston: Little, Brown, and Company.

Means, M. (2011). The Recipe for Ecstasy What Women Want: Sexual and relationship satisfaction. CreateSpace.com.

Metz, M. W. (2007). The "good-enough sex" model for couple sexual satisfaction. Sexual & Relationship Therapy, 22(3), 351-362.

Sternberg, R. J. (1986). A triangular theory of love. Psychological Review, 93, 119-135.

Sternberg, R. J. (1988). The Triangle of Love: Intimacy, passion, commitment. New York: Basic Books.

How to find Dr. Myrtle C. Means

Email: drmeans@therecipeforecstasy.com

Read my latest blog and find out about upcoming events on my Website:

www.therecipeforecstasy.com

Like The Recipe for Ecstasy on Facebook

Follow me on Twitter: @DrMeans

Follow me on Instagram: @DrMCMeans

Follow me on YouTube: The Recipe for Ecstasy

www.ingramcontent.com/pod-product-compliance
Lightning Source LLC
Chambersburg PA
CBHW082358270326
41935CB00013B/1670